THE NAKED TRUTH

SEXUAL PURITY FOR GUYS IN THE REAL WORLD

www.invertbooks.com

WWW.ZONDERVAN.COM

Bill Perkins and **Randy Southern**

Edited by Will Penner
Proofread by Laura Gross and Kristi Robison
Cover design by Burnkit
Interior design by Holly Sharp
Printed in the United States

04 05 06 07 08 09 / DC / 10 9 8 7 6 5 4 3 2 1

TABLE OF CONTENTS

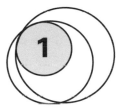

CHAPTER ONE

UNDERSTANDING WHY NAKED WOMEN LOOK SO GOOD

Can you imagine how freaked girls would be if they knew how guys really look at them?
—David A.

I don't get why people are so uptight about nudity. That's how God created us. I say if you've got it, show it off. I'm just talking about girls, though.
—Geoff V.

I think about girls a lot. I mean A LOT. Almost all the time. Do you think I have a problem?
—Vincente

·

The idea for this chapter came one Friday night while I was turning on my sprinkler system. As I walked across my yard, I noticed that my neighbor's lights were on. Curious as to why the neighbors were up so late, I approached the fence and looked through the slats. I expected to see a handful of people playing cards inside. Instead I saw a beautiful young woman talking on the phone. No big deal, right? Wrong.

The woman was naked.

Instantly my eyes locked on her. Adrenaline rushed through my body. My heart started pounding like a jackhammer. My breathing grew shallow. The rest of the world seemed to fade away as I focused on the unexpected sight before me.

After gazing at her for a few seconds, I managed to pry myself away from the fence. I walked away a little shaken and a lot curious—not about her, but about me. One question kept running through my mind: *Why did I have such an extreme reaction to the sight of a woman's body? Why did her naked beauty affect me so strongly?*

Maybe you've had a similar experience as an accidental peeping Tom. Or maybe your first exposure to female nudity came from a magazine. Or an adult Web site. Or some late-night movie on cable.

Whatever your experience was, I'll bet you remember your reaction to it. The question is: *Why* did you react that way? What is it about a naked woman that stops guys dead in our tracks? What is it about her that makes everything else suddenly seem uninteresting and unimportant?

Those are the questions I'm going to focus on in this first chapter. Once you understand *why* you react as you do, you can begin to explore healthy, God-pleasing ways to deal with your sexual feelings and urges.

A Work of Art

The first and most obvious reason guys react so strongly to the sight of a naked woman is that the female body is a masterpiece. Call it the crowning work of The Master Artist. Genesis 1 tells us that God created the universe, the earth, and all living creatures in six days.

Genesis 2:21-22 tells us that God put Adam, the first man, into a deep sleep. While Adam snoozed, God went to work on the final piece of creation: the woman. With careful precision and perfect artistry, God designed her eyes, her nose, her lips, her skin, her breasts, her hair, and—well, you get the idea. When Adam finally woke up, God's work was finished.

In human history there have been many momentous discoveries: Christopher Columbus discovering the New World, Ben Franklin discovering electricity, some guy named Reese discovering that chocolate and peanut butter taste great together. But none of them can compare to the discovery Adam made when he finally managed to stir from his slumber. Standing before him, in all of her God-created beauty and allure, was the first woman.

And she was naked.

The Bible doesn't tell us how Adam responded to such a glorious sight, but as a guy, you can probably imagine his reaction. In Genesis 2:23, Adam called his new companion "woman." The Hebrew word for "man" is *ish* and the Hebrew word for "woman" is *isha*. Perhaps when Adam got en eyeful of Eve, the first woman, he simply said "ish" and then added a moaning exclamation of awe and excitement: "aaaaaaaaaa!" If Adam had spoken English, he might have said, "Whoa! Man!"

Does a response like that make sense to you? As descendants of Adam, most of us experience the same extreme reaction to God's creative work in women. We share our ancestor's appreciation for the female form.

Want proof? The next time you're hanging out with a group of guys, toss out a question like this:

What's the most incredible sight in all of creation?

(a) The night sky during a meteor shower.
(b) A sunset in the Painted Desert.
(c) Twenty-foot waves off the coast of Maui.
(d) A fresh blanket of snow on the slopes of Vail.
(e) The female body.

Feel free to throw in any other natural wonders you can think of, but it probably won't change anyone's answer. As far as most guys are concerned, everything else in God's creation pales in comparison to the masterpiece of the female form.

The Hidden Treasure

Not only did Adam get to attend the unveiling of the first woman, but he also got to see her in *all* of her glory. Genesis 2:25 puts it this way: "The man and his wife were both naked, and they felt no shame."

Imagine having a beautiful naked woman by your side 24-7. Life was good for Adam...for a while. Unfortunately for him—

and for us—his time in paradise came to a screeching halt after one terrible decision. Ignoring God's clear warning, Adam and Eve decided that tasting the fruit of the forbidden tree was more interesting than obeying God's rules.

God's response was quick and severe. He booted Adam and Eve from the Garden of Eden and warned them that life was going to become extremely difficult and painful for them and their descendants.

Along with the pain of being separated from God and their home in the garden, Adam and Eve had to deal with a couple other new emotions: guilt and shame. One of the ways they dealt with their shame was to cover their naked bodies. Genesis 3:7 tells us they strung fig leaves around their hips to cover themselves. God later updated their wardrobe by giving them animal skins to wear (Genesis 3:21).

Just like that, the era of uninhibited nudity came to an end. And the modesty that began with Adam and Eve continues to this day.

That brings us to the second reason why the sight—or thought—of a naked woman has such an extreme effect on most guys: It's something we don't see very often. Nudity is a rare treat. Naked women get our attention because we seldom see them that way.

To take that concept one step further, you could say that the whole idea of nakedness is a special treat God has given only to human beings. To help you understand this concept, I offer the following true stories:

- In the late nineteenth century, a wealthy French woman dictated in her will that her entire fortune be used to buy clothes for the snowmen of Paris. That's right—snowmen. Apparently the woman found the sight of unclothed snowmen to be vulgar and offensive, so she determined to do something about it.

- In 1993, a supermarket chain in Dallas removed an issue of *Discover* magazine from its shelves because the cover showed a couple of nude apes.

- A European woman willed her entire estate to her niece on one condition: that the niece make sure the woman's pet goldfish wear pants at all times. That wasn't a misprint— the woman wanted her goldfish in trousers.

What led these people to make such odd decisions? Who knows? Whatever the reasons, though, it's safe to say that no one in his right mind would try to clothe a snowman or an ape or a goldfish. The fact is, those creatures can't be naked; our concept of "naked" involves the absence of clothes, and these creatures are never clothed in the first place.

How often do you put a shirt and pants on your cat before you let it out of the house? When was the last time you heard about a dog getting arrested for indecent exposure?

Nothing in creation is nude in the same sense that people are nude. Not trees, rocks, dogs, dolphins, or even the naked mole rat. No sane guy would ever be curious about the nakedness of an animal or a plant. Why would he be? Those things can't be naked.

Women, on the other hand, can be naked. Yet they seldom are. The females we see every day at school and at the mall and in the neighborhood all wear clothes. They cover themselves when they're around us. (Some girls cover more than others, of course, but we'll talk about that later in the book.) A naked woman, then, reveals what is almost always hidden from male eyes—the beauty of her body.

Comedian Tim Allen drives this point home in his description of the first time he saw a picture of a naked woman: "In a way, the picture was both frightening and reassuring. I realized for the first time that, dumb as it sounds, *all women are naked under their clothes*...That discovery made me distrust all women forever: they're hiding this! They have this power and I didn't even know it. It's just under their clothes!"

Allen raises a question that most guys can identify with. Namely, how can women walk around every day hiding something so wonderful? Not only that, how can they pretend they don't even know what they're doing? Don't they understand that the more they hide their nakedness, the more guys want to see it?

Curiosity may have killed the cat, but it also inspires all kinds of male fantasies.

The Completer

Don't get the wrong impression, though. As guys, our appreciation of the female form isn't as superficial and shallow as it may seem. It's not just a matter of physical lust. Our attraction to a woman's body goes a lot deeper than that. As a matter of fact, it can be traced back to the earliest days of creation.

Let's head back to Genesis 1 to find out where our overwhelming appreciation comes from. You'll notice that after each day of creation, God looked around at what he had made and announced that it was "good." Except for one thing. You'll find it in Genesis 2:18. God saw that Adam was alone, and he determined to do something about it.

Step One of his plan was to help Adam recognize that he needed someone. In order to do that, God gave Adam an assignment: to name all of the animals. We don't know how long the job took, but when you consider the variety of creatures in the world, it's not hard to imagine Adam spending months—maybe even years—naming them.

Although the Bible doesn't say so, it seems logical to assume that at some point in the process, Adam must have noticed that the animals came in pairs, male and female. He also must have noticed that none of the creatures God paraded past him resembled him in any way. None of them eased his loneliness.

How long do you think it took before this started to bother him? Imagine how alone Adam must have felt as the final animals filed past him and he realized that everything in creation had a partner but him.

When Adam's feelings of aloneness started to get intense, God stepped in. As I mentioned earlier, he put Adam into a deep sleep and performed the first act of surgery. He took a rib from Adam's side and custom-made a companion for him. Just as the first man was made from the earth, the first woman was made from the man.

With the creation of Eve, Adam lost a rib. With the appearance of Eve, Adam discovered the one who would make him complete. Without her, Adam was like a pen without ink or a ship without a sail—he was incomplete. Part of him was missing—literally. He needed Eve to complete him.

As descendants of Adam, most guys have that same need

and that same sense of incompleteness. That's the way we've been created. I'm not talking about a surface emotion here. You may not *feel* incomplete. The need I'm talking about exists at the deepest part of our being. It's there because God put it there. He gave us a need that can only be satisfied by a woman. To put it another way: Women fill up what's lacking in guys.

Isn't it possible, then, that the beauty of a woman's body is somehow linked to our need for completeness? The Bible doesn't say this, but maybe at the deepest level of our subconscious, we have a craving for someone who will make us whole in the way God intended.

Maybe our desire for someone who will make us complete is what causes us to react as we do to a woman's body. Perhaps in the moment when a guy gazes at a woman's naked beauty, he experiences—for a fleeting second—the hope of being whole.

Getting Intimate

We can't talk about nakedness without mentioning intimacy. Intimacy is what makes nudity special. When God designed us as sexual beings, he put intimacy and trust at the heart of the male-female relationship. A woman who takes off her clothes in front of a guy is putting her trust in him. She makes herself vulnerable. She allows him to see not just her beauty, but her flaws as well. That kind of intimacy requires a special relationship, which can only occur between people who love and accept each other, warts and all.

Adam and Eve had such intimacy. After God brought them together, they "felt no shame" (Genesis 2:25), even though they were completely nude. Their physical nakedness matched the nakedness that existed at a deeper level—a spiritual and emotional level. Adam and Eve were intimate in every sense of the word.

If you're like most guys, you probably don't consider yourself a prime candidate for intimacy. The idea of completely opening up to someone may make your skin crawl. But while most guys shy away from intimacy, we still need it. The problem is, we've been programmed to believe we have to be self-sufficient. Since childhood we've bought into the lie that "real" men are independent and rugged. That they never need anyone's help. That they never share their inner feelings with anyone.

That attitude may work for fictional action heroes, but not for flesh-and-blood guys. No matter how much we try to tell ourselves that we can make it alone in this world, something inside us screams for an intimate connection at the deepest level. I believe naked women are beautiful to us because their nakedness tells us, "I'm here for you. I'm yours. I've made myself bare for your eyes." That tells a man he's safe. It tells him he's loved. It tells him someone wants to be intimate with him.

Because nakedness involves intimacy, seeing a naked woman provides guys with an intimate connection—even if it's a superficial one. However, *true* intimacy can only occur in a safe setting, in an environment of love and trust.

Good News

Before I wrap up this chapter, I need to make one more extremely important point about the female body and our reaction to it: There's no reason for you to feel like a pervert because you enjoy the sight (or thought) of the female form. God gave you your sexual appetite. He created the pleasure centers in your body; he designed your body to react the way it does when you get turned on; and he wired you with a strong physical attraction to female flesh.

That may come as a shock to people who think of God as being anti-sex. But saying that God opposes sex is like saying he opposes marriage or church; it's ridiculous. Forget Hugh Hefner or Dr. Drew or any other so-called "sexpert." God is the biggest supporter of sex you'll ever find. In fact, God doesn't just support human sex—he actually *celebrates* it.

If you have a hard time believing that, check out a little book in the Old Testament called Song of Songs (or Song of Solomon, depending on which biblical translation you use). At first glance this book seems out of place in Scripture: King Solomon and his bride take turns reciting love poems to each other. And let's just say these two lovebirds weren't shy about expressing their passion for one another.

Check out this passage from the book:

You have stolen my heart, my sister, my bride; you have stolen my heart with one glance of your eyes, with one jewel of your necklace. How delightful is your love, my sister, my bride! How much more pleasing is your love than wine, and the fragrance of your perfume than any spice! Your lips drop sweetness as the honeycomb, my bride; milk and honey are under your tongue. The fragrance of your garments is like that of Lebanon. (Song of Songs 4:9-11)

Welcome to the first night of the honeymoon! Once the two lovers are alone, the king tells his bride that the look in her eyes is enough to excite him. You know the kind of look he's talking about, don't you?

Solomon also uses a familiar image to get his point across.

The area where the Jewish people lived was often described as "the land of milk and honey." The land offered great richness and pleasure to those who lived in it. In a similar way, the woman Solomon held in his arms provided him with both pleasure and well-being.

Here's another passage from the book:

You are a garden locked up, my sister, my bride; you are a spring enclosed, a sealed fountain. Your plants are an orchard of pomegranates with choice fruits, with henna and nard, nard and saffron, calamus and cinnamon, with every kind of incense tree, with myrrh and aloes and all the finest spices. You are a garden fountain, a well of flowing water streaming down from Lebanon. (Song of Songs 4:12-15)

Maybe you appreciate Solomon's poetry; maybe you don't. But if you look beyond all the fruit and spice references, you'll see that Solomon is talking about his bride's virginity. He points out that her fountain is his alone and her garden is private. In other words, no one has ever entered her before. But now the night for a visitor has arrived, and Solomon is seriously stoked to be that visitor. That's why he goes into such detail about the aroma and taste of her love.

Solomon's not the only one getting aroused in this passage. The fact that his bride's fountain has become a "well of flowing water" (verse 15) suggests that she's pretty excited as well. She makes that clear in verse 16 when she invites Solomon to "come into his garden and taste its choice fruits."

Whoa. Is it getting hot in here?

The point is that I'm not quoting from some ancient book of erotic writings; it's the *Bible*. God chose to include these passages for us; God wants us to read these words of passion. He gives us a peek into Solomon's honeymoon suite to help us understand just how incredible sex can be—when the circumstances are right.

The Ultimate Playground

Speaking of those "right" circumstances, here's how cool God is— not only did he create guys so that we get pleasure from playing with a naked woman, but he also created the ideal playground for us. It's called marriage.

God intends sex to be one of the most powerful and pleasurable experiences of life. It's when a man and woman become "one flesh." Their bodies literally are linked together. During those incredible moments, the man and the one created from him become whole again. They are one.

God's plan is for this oneness to take place within the safety of marriage because marriage is the only place where true intimacy, security, and commitment can exist between a guy and a girl. Couples who exchange marriage vows commit themselves to developing the kind of intimacy that nakedness requires. Marriage, then, is the only place in which a guy can totally celebrate and enjoy the beauty of a woman's body.

Of course, the fact that God wants sex to take place in marriage creates a world of challenges for guys who aren't married yet. I'll tackle those challenges in the chapters that follow.

Getting Personal

1. When was the first time you saw naked female flesh? (I'm talking about when you were old enough to appreciate it.) How did you react?

2. In your opinion what's the best thing about the way God created guys and girls? Why?

3. What would you like to say to God about his work in creating the female body? What would you like to say to him about his gift of sex?

CHAPTER TWO

WAITING...AND WAITING...
AND WAITING...

If you're a guy, you're supposed to hit your sexual peak when you're, like, 18 or something. That means if you wait until you're married, you'll miss out on the best sex of your life!
—Kelly

My brother says being horny is like being hungry or thirsty. It's natural. There's nothing wrong with it.
—Orlando

I know a lot of guys who've had sex. It didn't ruin their lives. It just made things more fun.
—Zach

Imagine this scenario:

You're 13 years old, and you're a car freak. Your friends are into cars, too, and that's practically all you talk about. You admire rides on the street. You check them out in magazines and Web sites. You draw pictures of them in school. You've got car fever.

One day you open your garage door to take out the trash, and there it is. The sweetest, sleekest, fastest-looking car you've ever seen. At least that's the way you imagine it looks. The car itself is under a big drop cloth. So though you can't actually tell what it's like, you know it's something spectacular. And the best part—it's parked right there in your own garage!

Just then your parents walk in with big smiles on their faces. "How do you like it?" your dad asks. You just grin at him. "Good," he says, "because it's yours." Your jaw hits the floor.

"Your father and I love you very much," your mom explains. "And we know how happy this car will make you. So we want you to have it."

But then your dad throws in the kicker: "It's yours to drive—as soon as you turn 25."

Your smile fades. "Twenty-five? That's 12 years from now!" you protest. "I'll be old enough to drive in three years!"

"We understand that," your parents reply. "But trust us, if you wait until after high school and college, you'll appreciate the car a lot more. You won't be as tempted to drive it recklessly. Plus, your insurance rates will be a lot lower."

While you stare in amazement, your parents lay out the

ground rules. The car will be kept in the garage, under its protective covering, until your 25th birthday. Then it will be yours to enjoy for the rest of your life.

What would you think of a gift like that? How hard would it be to accept your parents' terms? Before you answer, let's flash-forward a few years. You've got your driver's license. As far as the law's concerned, you're free to drive your car anytime you want. But your parents won't budge on their terms.

To make matters worse, a lot of your friends are starting to get cars of their own. They talk about how much fun it is to tool around. They brag about what good drivers they are. And, of course, they make fun of you for not driving your car.

When you get a girlfriend, the situation becomes more urgent. She starts dropping hints about how nice it would be if the two of you could go for a drive in your car. You manage to make excuses for a while, but she keeps getting more insistent. At one point she tells you that if you really love her, you'll ignore your parents' rules and take her for a ride in the car.

Adding to your pressure is the fact that everywhere you look—TV, movies, magazines, music videos, billboards—you see people enjoying their cars. And every scene reminds you that you can't join in the fun yet.

Under those conditions, no one would blame you if you started to question your parents' guidelines, would they? Or if you started to spend more time in the garage, peeking under the car cover, taking a look at what's waiting for you.

But the excitement of peeking would last only so long. At some point you'd want to take the cover off completely to get a better look at your car. And then you'd want to open the door and climb behind the wheel. Of course, you'd also want to hear what the car sounds like. So when the time's right, you'd jump in and fire up the engine. Maybe you'd rev it a few times, just to feel its awesome power.

After a while, though, even that thrill would fade. And then you'd be faced with your biggest decision of all: Do you blow off your parents' wishes and start enjoying your present whenever you get the urge to drive, or do you resist temptation? Do you listen to what your parents tell you and keep the car in the garage until your 25th birthday—even if it means waiting nine more years?

Taking the car out would give you a lot of immediate pleasure. It might also make you popular with your friends—not to mention your dates. But it would hurt your parents, the ones who loved you enough to give you the gift in the first place.

Quite a dilemma, isn't it?

The Gift

James 1:17 makes it clear that "Every good and perfect gift is from above, coming down from the Father of the heavenly lights." Sex certainly fits into that category. It may not be *perfect,* but it's definitely good. And you have God to thank for it. Like the parents in the story, God has given you an incredible gift—that is, the ability to experience sexual pleasure—because he loves you. He wants you to enjoy the intense excitement and satisfaction that comes from having sex.

Like the parents in the story, God has laid out some requirements for using his gift. Specifically, he wants you to wait until you're married to unwrap it. As the apostle Paul puts it, "each man should have his own wife, and each woman her own husband" (1 Corinthians 7:2). As far as God's concerned, sex is an exclusive treat for husbands and wives.

As I mentioned in chapter 1, that requirement creates a tricky situation for sexual wannabes. Statistics show that most guys get married in their early to mid-20s. However, most guys start experiencing intense sexual urges in their early to mid-teens—sometimes even before that. That's a difference of at least 10 years.

And 10 years is a *looo-oo-ooong* time.

What happens to your sex drive in the meantime? It doesn't go away, that's for sure. God's already given you the gift—the ability to experience sexual pleasure. He's not going to take it back until your wedding day. So it sits in limbo, in the "garage" of your life, waiting for the day it can be used.

But it's still available to you.

You have access to your gift 24-7. And if you're like most guys, it's never very far from your mind.

As if that's not tempting enough, you live in a culture that doesn't seem to care about God's guidelines for your gift. Think about it—what was the last movie you saw that didn't have a sex scene in it? What was the last TV show you watched that didn't have people talking about getting some—or not getting some? How often do you see hot girls in music videos or commercials who look and act as though they'd like nothing better than to have sex?

And then you've got the guys at school. The ones who can make a sex joke out of *anything* anyone says. The ones who insist on showing you their latest downloaded porn. The ones who like to talk about every single detail of their grope sessions. The ones who make fun of you because you haven't scored yet.

When you get a girlfriend—or even when you start hanging out with girls—the situation gets worse. Sooner or later you're going to run into girls who like to mess around. And if you're in the right place at the right time, you're going to have a chance to get what you've been dreaming about since you hit puberty.

With all that pressure, who could blame you if you started to question God's instructions? If you started to wonder whether saving sex for marriage is really worth the trouble. If you started to get frustrated about your unsatisfied urges. If you started to develop a burning desire to "peek under the cover" of God's gift to you.

Let's say you give in to that desire, and you start to explore your ability to experience sexual pleasure. Like the example of the car in the analogy, the first few times will seem harmless. You may tell yourself it's just natural curiosity. Maybe you'll check out a few Web sites or flip through a friend's porno stash. That'll satisfy your curiosity for a while...but not for long.

So you'll move on to the next step. You'll get a little more risky. Maybe you'll start downloading your own porno stash. Somewhere along the way, you'll start masturbating. You'll learn to take care of your own needs when the urge hits you. You can think of that as getting behind the wheel of your car and starting the engine to get the feel for what driving is like. That'll keep you occupied for a while. But it won't satisfy you—not for more than a few minutes at a time, at least.

Looking at the same old images will get boring. Your relationship with your hand will lose its excitement. So you'll start looking for other ways to satisfy yourself. Better ways. Ways that involve real live girls.

And then you'll be faced with the dilemma Christian guys have faced for centuries. You've got one of the greatest gifts in the world within your reach. You have the ability to unwrap it and use it anytime you want. But you also know what God expects of you. You know how important it is to him that you follow his instructions. You know if you misuse what he's given you, you'll disappoint him. You know it will hurt your relationship with him. And you know it will spoil his plan for your wedding night.

In other words, you've got the equipment. You've got the urges. You've got the opportunities. But you don't have permission from the only One whose opinion really matters.

What should you do?

A Once-in-a-Lifetime Opportunity

If you've grown up in a traditional church, you know the answer that's coming. If you've read any Christian magazine articles or books or watched any Christian videos about sex, you know I'm going to tell you how important it is to resist temptation. You know I'm going to tell you that if you save yourself for marriage, you'll always be glad you did. You know I'm going to emphasize how important it is to follow God's plan in dealing with your sexual urges.

Before I do that, though, I want to tackle a question many Christian guys struggle with but are afraid to ask: *Since God gave guys hormones that kick in before high school, why doesn't he want us to experience sex until after we're married?*

It's a fair question. Unfortunately, the Bible doesn't give us a lot of behind-the-scenes looks at God's creative process. You won't find a verse that explains why he made our bodies as he did. But you will find some passages that throw a whole new light on this idea of life before marriage and sex.

Let's start with Romans 12:1. That's where the apostle Paul says, "Therefore, I urge you, brothers, in view of God's mercy, to offer your bodies as living sacrifices, holy and pleasing to God— this is your spiritual act of worship." A sacrifice is something people offer to God to show their faithfulness. What does that have to do with a guy's body?

Paul answers that question in 1 Corinthians 7:32-33: "I would like you to be free from concern. An unmarried man is concerned about the Lord's affairs—how he can please the Lord. But a married man is concerned about the affairs of this world— how he can please his wife."

God isn't punishing you by making you wait for sex. He's giving you an incredible opportunity. You have a window of about 10 years between puberty and marriage to offer an awesome sacrifice to God—with your body.

You have the ability to bring honor to God in a way that married guys can't. It's all about how you use your body. The things you do with it. And the things you refuse to do with it. You can be a living sacrifice by resisting the temptations that bombard you every day, by battling the urges that constantly hound you, and by refusing to choose temporary pleasure over lifetime devotion.

Of course you'll still be able to honor God when you're married. And your body can still be a living sacrifice to him. But it won't be the same. Your responsibilities as a husband—and later as a father—will demand your attention. And your ability to serve God will be changed.

Here is the bottom line—you have an amazing opportunity staring you in the face. An opportunity you'll never have again in your life. Don't let it slip away. Because all the orgasms in the world can't match the thrill you could have one day when God looks you in the eyes—with all of Heaven looking on—and says, "Well done, good and faithful servant!...Come and share your master's happiness!" (Matthew 25:21).

Know Your Enemy

If you decide to accept the challenge of making your body a living sacrifice, not everyone will be rooting for you to succeed. In fact, you can count on one enemy to do everything in his power to make sure you fail.

He's Satan, the devil. And the Bible describes him as "a roaring lion looking for someone to devour" (1 Peter 5:8). He doesn't just want to stop you. He wants to take you out of the game completely.

The last thing in the world the devil needs is a young guy whose relationship with God is more important to him than anything else. The idea of offering your body as a living sacrifice scares him because he knows the incredible things that can come from it.

That's why he'll use every weapon he has to stop you. For example, he may use doubt to get inside your head and make you question God's Word. It's a trick he's used before. Look back at the story of Adam and Eve in Genesis 3. Check out the question the serpent (Satan) threw at Eve: "Did God really say…?"

He'll use the same kind of questions with you:

- Did God really say not to have sex before marriage? Isn't that just some people's interpretation of the Bible?
- Is it really wrong to have sex with a girl you truly care about? Why do you need a ring and a marriage license to prove your love?
- Isn't God's plan unfair to people who never get married? Does that mean they never get to find out what sex is like?
- Does God really expect you to stay sexually frustrated until your wedding day? How can sex be any good after you get married if you've never had any practice?

If your enemy can make you start to doubt God's plan, he can chip away at your commitment. (By the way, I've done an extensive study of the Bible, and I've never found a loophole around God's command that we be sexually pure.)

And if all else fails, your enemy can haul out the Big Gun.

The "L" Word

Lust is the dark side of God's gift of sex. It's the twisted version of your natural appreciation for the female form. Lust is what causes you to stop thinking of girls as people and start thinking of them as sex objects. Playthings to be used and forgotten.

What's dangerous about lust is that it's fueled by things that are off-limits. The more someone tells you that you can't have something, the more you're going to lust after it. And the harder you try to keep your lust in check, the harder Satan's going to try to set it free. He'll use magazine covers, beer commercials, music videos, morning radio shows, online pop-up ads, and girls at school who like to show some skin. Anything that will make you stop thinking about your sacrifice to God—and start thinking about feeding your lust.

So how do you battle an enemy like Satan who has access to a weapon as powerful as lust? That's what the rest of this book will explain. In the meantime, though, we're going to end this chapter with a story that illustrates the key to success when it comes to dealing with lust.

The Incurable Itch

Once upon a time, a young man moved into a cave in the mountains to study with a wise man. The student wanted to learn everything there was to know. The wise man supplied him with stacks of books. Then before the wise man left the cave, he sprinkled a powder on the man's hand that caused him to itch.

Every morning the wise man returned to the cave to monitor his student's progress. "Have you learned everything there is to know yet?" the wise man asked.

And every morning his student's answer was the same: "No, I haven't."

The wise man then sprinkled more itching powder on his student's hand and left.

The scenario was repeated for months. One day the wise man entered the cave, but before he could ask his question, the student reached out, grabbed the bag of powder, and tossed it into the fire.

"Congratulations," the wise man said, much to his student's

surprise. "You have graduated. You know everything you need to know."

"How's that?" the student asked.

"You have learned that you don't have to wait until you've learned everything before you can do something positive," he replied. "And you have learned how to take control of your life and stop the itching."

Be like the student in this story. Take the fight to Satan. Don't wait for him to put things in front of you and then try to react to them. Disarm him before he gets a chance to attack.

Don't let anything spoil the awesome gift that's waiting for you.

Getting Personal

1. How do you feel about the gift God's given you? How do you feel about waiting for years to enjoy it?

2. What steps can you take to make your body the kind of sacrifice that will please God?

3. What's your most vulnerable area when it comes to lust? How can you prevent your enemy from attacking you there?

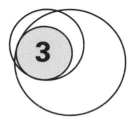

CHAPTER THREE

MARKING THE LINES

Premarital sex won't be a problem for me. I have a lot of self-control.
—Wynn

If God created sex, how can it be bad?
—Nas

Should I feel guilty about masturbating?
—Olin

You and your friends want to play some pickup football (touch, flag, tackle—whatever you prefer). You've got a ball. You've got a wide-open place to play. And you've got even teams.

Before you start the game, though, there's one important thing you have to do. You have to set your boundaries—sidelines, goal lines, and end lines. You have to determine what's inbounds and what's out-of-bounds.

You could try playing without boundary lines, but things would probably get frustrating and confusing pretty quickly. If you're going to play the game right, you need to know how far you can go. You need to know how much room you have to work with.

The same goes for sex.

What Do You Mean by "Sex"?

God's plan is for guys and girls to save sex until marriage. (That sound you hear is millions of Christian parents and church leaders nodding their heads in agreement.) But that leads to a pretty obvious question: What *is* sex? And what, exactly, are you supposed to *save*?

To put it in football terms, where are the boundary lines? How much room do you have to work with? How far can you go? (That sound you hear is millions of Christian parents and church leaders going, "Um, um…")

It's not like there's a shortage of opinions on the subject. Lots of Christian guys have set boundaries for themselves, sexually speaking. The problem is finding agreement on where those boundaries belong.

Tony
When the Bible talks about sex, it's talking about intercourse. Or whatever you want to call it. That's what "two people becoming one flesh" means. That's what I'm saving for marriage. So if somebody asks me if I'm a virgin, I say yes. Even though I've had oral sex and stuff like that. Because those things don't count. They're not really sex.

Luis
I think there's a difference between teasing and sex. Teasing is when you're just messing around. You know, exploring bodies and stuff. How else are you gonna learn? You've gotta find out what feels good to a girl. Otherwise your wife's gonna be bummed on your wedding night. I say as long as you don't have an orgasm, it's not really sex.

Justin
I believe there's a difference between having sex and making love. I don't think God wants people doing it just because they feel like it or because they're drunk or whatever. But if you love someone, it's different. Then it's making love. It's something beautiful instead of something sleazy.

Michael
I think it depends on the person. There are some things I can do and not feel guilty about. But if another guy does the same thing, he might feel guilty. You have to be true to yourself. Don't make decisions based on what other people do or what other people tell you is right. Do what's right for you—and the person you love.

Shon
I don't really have a choice. My girlfriend won't let me do anything more than kiss her. I tried to get a little more a couple times, but she threatened to dump me. So now I'm a good boy. Well...almost. I told her I'd do the kissing thing. But I also told

her she had to make it worth my while. And she has. She's a great kisser.

Kip
I made a pledge to save sex for marriage. To me that means not doing anything with a girl that I wouldn't want my future wife doing with another guy. I know it sounds weird. Especially since I have no clue who my future wife will be. But it just seems fair, you know?

How do your views of what's "too far" compare with these? How would you explain your boundaries when it comes to sex?

How do you think God feels about your boundaries? Think carefully before you answer. Raging hormones and wishful thinking have been known to cloud guys' judgments. With enough incentive, you could justify an orgy. And if you're really good, you could even make it sound biblical.

But God isn't swayed by lame excuses or desperate rationalizations. And fooling yourself is never a good idea, especially when the stakes are so high.

Myth Busting

So how does an unmarried guy like you come up with a clear guideline for his love life? How can you enjoy the pleasures of the opposite sex without misusing your body?

You can start by finding out for yourself what God expects of you. You'd be surprised by how many well-meaning Christian guys have set sexual standards for themselves based on myths and mistaken ways of thinking when it comes to God and his Word. To help you avoid that mistake, let's take a look at three of the most common myths that can trip you up.

Myth #1: *The Bible's silence is our gain.*

You can search every book of the Bible and not find a verse that says oral sex before marriage is a sin. Nor will you find a passage about undressing a girl or tongue kissing. In fact, you won't find many specific guidelines about what's okay and what's not for sexually curious guys.

Some people use this fact to support the argument that (almost) anything goes. Their attitude is: If the Bible doesn't outlaw it, I'm allowed to do it.

The problem with this line of thinking, however, is that it assumes the Bible is nothing more than a rule book. A list of *do's* and *don'ts*. A fat book with countless ways God wants to ground us. And that's a really lame way to look at God's Word.

The Bible is actually more like a treasure map. A detailed plan for discovering the awesome things God has planned for you. A guide for making the best possible choices for yourself in every situation.

There's an old story about comedian W.C. Fields, who was quite well-known for his drinking, fooling around, and unwise lifestyle choices. Toward the end of his life—while Fields was living in a sanatorium—a friend entered his room and found Fields thumbing through a Bible. The friend was astonished. "Bill, I've never seen you with a Bible or within a mile of a church. What are you doing?" he asked.

"Looking for loopholes," Fields answered.

That story's kind of amusing as a joke, but it's tragic as a human episode. Now, if you are looking for loopholes in God's Word, you're missing about 99.9 percent of what it has to offer.

Besides, the Bible isn't nearly as silent on sexual matters as some people would like to believe. You can find plenty of clues scattered throughout Scripture that reveal God's attitude toward sexual experimentation.

One of the first clues can be found in 1 Corinthians 6:18: "Flee from sexual immorality. All other sins a man commits are outside his body, but he who sins sexually sins against his own body."

Look at that first sentence again. *Run away from sexual immorality.* Think of it as a ticking bomb at the beginning of an action movie. The people who see it and run away as fast as they can will probably survive. But the arrogant "expert" who thinks he can defuse it by himself will end up getting smeared across the room.

That's the kind of danger sexual temptation presents. If you're conceited enough to believe you can mess around with it safely, you're in for a nasty surprise. It's a matter of direction: if you're running away from sexual temptation, you're heading in one direction. If you're trying to see how close you can get to the boundary line without going over, you're heading in the opposite direction. And you have to admit that doing the opposite of what God commands is *always* a bad idea.

Clue number two can be found a few books later in the New Testament: "But among you there must not be even a hint of sexual immorality, or of any kind of impurity, or of greed, because these are improper for God's holy people." That's what Ephesians 5:3 says. *Not even a hint.* Talk about setting the bar high!

Guys can make all the pitches they want about why certain things technically shouldn't be considered sex. But if those things have even a *hint* of sexual immorality, they're off limits. Ephesians 5:3 makes that crystal clear.

And then there's clue number three, which comes courtesy of Colossians 3:5: "Put to death, therefore, whatever belongs to your earthly nature: sexual immorality, impurity, lust, evil desires and greed, which is idolatry."

That doesn't sound like a God who's wishy-washy when it comes to his people playing around with sex. As far as he's concerned, you're in a fight to the finish with sexual sin. If you don't destroy it, it will destroy you. No matter how harmless it may seem right now.

Like it or not, God isn't going to spoon-feed you every bit of information you need to stay sexually pure. He's not going to supernaturally highlight every relevant verse in your Bible. Discovering his truth is your job. And it's not always an easy thing to do. Especially with so many other so-called truths competing for your attention. But if you commit yourself to learning what his Word says about sexual purity, he will help you discover his truth.

Myth #2: Setting sexual boundaries for yourself will take care of your problem.

Don't get me wrong. When it comes to sex, setting physical limits for yourself is a great idea. Especially if you commit yourself to respecting those limits. But it won't solve your problem completely.

You see, your fight isn't just physical; it's mental and spiritual, too. Jesus made that clear when he said, "But I tell you that anyone who looks at a woman lustfully has already committed adultery with her in his heart" (Matthew 5:28). How's that for a standard?

You can keep your pants zipped from now until your wedding day, but it won't keep you safe from sexual sin. The male imagination is a state-of-the-art, industrial-strength machine—especially when it's churning out sexual fantasies. Guys are ingenious when it comes to imagining erotic scenarios. There's no situation we can't turn into a sexual one if we just put our minds to it. So no matter where you draw the line physically, you still have to contend with your eyes and your thoughts.

Myth #3: More than anything else, God's wants us to enjoy his gift of sex.

Don't be fooled into thinking that your enjoyment is at the top of God's priority list. It's not. "It is God's will that you should be sanctified: that you should avoid sexual immorality; that each of you should learn to control his own body in a way that is holy and honorable, not in passionate lust like the heathen, who do not know God...For God did not call us to be impure, but to live a holy life." I didn't say that; the apostle Paul did in 1 Thessalonians 4:3-5, 7.

God wants you to be pure. He wants you to obey him. He wants you to honor him in the things you do and say. He wants you to live your life as an example to others. That's what God wants. You can certainly enjoy yourself doing those things. But enjoyment isn't your ultimate goal—not if you're serious about living a life that pleases God.

You see, this isn't about getting what you want. It's about giving up what you want—for God's sake. "Do you not know that your body is a temple of the Holy Spirit, who is in you, whom you have received from God? You are not your own; you were bought at a price. Therefore honor God with your body." Those are Paul's words again, from 1 Corinthians 6:19-20.

God has a purpose for you. And getting as much as you can from girls isn't part of it. Living a holy life is a 24-7 commitment. You can't call time-out, go mess around for a while, and then come back to it. To be holy you have to completely change your perspective on satisfying your urges.

That doesn't mean you have to live like a monk and shut yourself off from the world. God's not boring! As I mentioned in chapter 1, he's the One who created the pleasure centers in your body. But living a holy life does mean you have to learn to say no to your body—even when it's screaming for action.

Guarding the Line

If you want to set boundaries for yourself, don't think in terms of first base, second base, and third base. Because no matter what you tell yourself before the game, when you're on the field, sooner or later you're going to try to stretch a single into a double. Or steal a base, if you can get away with it. That's the way lust works at the ol' ball game.

Instead set your boundaries with God. Lust begins when you stop trying to please him with your body and start trying to please yourself. So make that your boundary line—the moment you stop thinking about living in a holy way and start thinking about satisfying a sexual urge. Whether it happens while you're kissing, hugging, holding hands, or staring at the girl who sits in front of you, that's the moment you need to hit the brakes and do a 180.

If that means ending a date early, do it.

If it means not hanging out with certain girls, do it.

If it means asking God every five minutes to help you control your eyes and thoughts, do it.

It's that important.

Besides, whatever sacrifices you have to make to live a holy life will pale in comparison to the reward God has waiting for you. You take good care of your body now, and God will make it worth your while in a big way later.

The "Contest"

Setting sexual guidelines for couples is only half the battle. Maybe even less, since not all guys with sexual urges are dating. The other part of the equation applies to almost every one of us.

Masturbation. Solo sex. Self-pleasure. Call it what you want. In the land of guys' sexual issues, masturbation is king. Remember the old *Seinfeld* episode called "The Contest"? The one where Jerry and his friends have trouble abstaining from masturbation? That may be funny when it happens to fictional characters, but it's not funny when it happens to real people.

Recently, a one-armed man approached me after a question-and-answer session at a men's event. He held out his left hand, the only one he had, and said with a glimmer in his eyes, "Is it true that if you masturbate, hair grows on your hands?"

As I looked at his hairless left hand, I said, "No. But I'll tell you what does happen."

"What's that?" he asked.

"They lose the arm they masturbate with."

The guy bent over in laughter. I smiled and said, "It's a good thing that's not the consequence of masturbation because we'd all be armless."

Let's all agree right now. Everyone with an arm and a hand masturbates at one time or another. I've heard it said that 95 percent of guys admit they've masturbated and the other 5 percent have a habit of lying. Whether that's true or not, there's no question that it's much more common than most of us would like to think.

But is masturbation wrong?

Back in the day, parents used to warn their sons that masturbation caused blindness. And in response to this dire prediction an entire generation of guys replied, "Okay, then we'll just do it until we need glasses." Medical science (not to mention the relentless research of billions of guys around the world) has disproved that theory. But the stigma remains. Most guys are raised to believe that masturbation is something to be ashamed of.

But is it a sin?

You won't find a specific passage in the Bible to answer the question for you. Believe me, I've searched from cover to cover.

Christian leaders can't even agree on the topic. Some of them teach that masturbation is a gift from God, a healthy way to relieve sexual pressure before marriage. Others argue that masturbation encourages lust and therefore can't be considered a moral thing to do.

Some people have tried to use the story of Onan in Genesis 38 to prove that God opposes masturbation. It's not a well-known story, so I'll give you the highlights of it: In Old Testament times, if a husband died before he had a son, his younger brother would marry his widow. That's what happened to Onan. His older brother Er died, and he had to marry Tamar, Er's widow. According to God's law, if Onan and Tamar had a son, he would be considered Er's heir. (Having an heir was a big deal in Old Testament times.)

Onan was afraid that having a son with Tamar would interfere with his own heir-raising plans. So when he had sex with Tamar, he pulled out just prior to climax and finished himself off, spilling his semen on the ground. God considered that a wicked thing to do and struck Onan dead.

But if you look at the passage closely, you'll see that God didn't punish Onan for masturbating; he punished him for using Tamar to satisfy his sexual urges without fulfilling his responsibility to his brother.

So where does that leave us?

Maybe the best way to deal with this topic is to say that masturbation is amoral at best. At worst, it clearly can be wrong.

Your challenge, once again, is to figure out where the line is. In order to do that, you need to answer three questions:

1. What are you thinking about?

Remember Jesus' words in Matthew 5:28: "But I tell you that anyone who looks at a woman lustfully has already committed adultery with her in his heart." Even though masturbation technically may not be considered a sin, fantasizing about women—imagining yourself having sex with them—clearly is. And it's pretty hard to separate one from the other.

Don't even bother asking if Jesus' warning includes porn. Of course it does. The whole purpose of porn is to get you lusting. And not *just* porn, either. Jesus' words apply to any masturbation material you use: Victoria's Secret catalogs, MTV Spring Break shows, yearbook photos, or whatever.

It's not the act of masturbation that causes you problems; it's the thoughts and fantasies that go with it. If you can't control your thoughts while masturbating, you've crossed the line.

2. How much control do you have over your masturbating?

Occasional masturbation might be one thing. But obsessive masturbation is a serious problem. Several years ago a young man told me he masturbated four or five times a day. His entire life revolved around when and where he would masturbate. That may be an extreme example, but there are a lot of guys who find they can't resist the urge to masturbate.

In 1 Corinthians 6:12, Paul says, "'Everything is permissible for me'—but not everything is beneficial. 'Everything is permissible for me'—but I will not be mastered by anything."

That's what happens when masturbation gets out of control. You become a slave to your own sex drive. And that's not an option for someone who wants to live a holy life.

If masturbation takes up a big chunk of your alone time, you've crossed the line. If you say no to social invitations so you can stay home and masturbate, you've crossed the line. If you think about masturbating a lot at church, school, or other inappropriate places, you've crossed the line. If you can't say no to the urge to masturbate, you've crossed the line.

3. What's it doing to your view of sex?

No matter how good masturbation feels, it's an extremely poor substitute for the real thing. That's important to keep in mind because God has something really good in store for you. And if you're willing to settle for the extremely temporary thrills of masturbation, you won't be able to appreciate his incredible gift when you get married. And that's a real problem. So if you start to confuse masturbation with what sex should really feel like, you've crossed the line.

What it comes down to is this: If you can honestly say to God—

- "I'm not dwelling on lustful thoughts";
- "I'm in control of my behavior, and I'm not a slave to my urges"; and
- "I'm not negatively affecting my view of sex"

—then occasional masturbation may help you keep your sexual frustrations under control.

But if you can't honestly say those things, you need to rethink your relationship with your hand. It's spoiling your chance to offer your body as a sacrifice to God and to live a life that pleases him.

Getting Personal

1. How do you think your friends would define their sexual boundaries? How much have their attitudes toward sex affected yours?

2. On a scale of 1 to 10, how pleased do you think God is with your current sexual boundaries? What are the primary things you need to do in order to raise that number to a 10?

3. Which of the three masturbation questions was the most difficult for you to answer truthfully? Why?

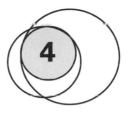

CHAPTER FOUR

ESCAPING FROM SEXUAL TRAPS

My sex-ed teacher says masturbation is natural and healthy for guys my age. So why do I feel weird when I do it?
—Derek

I asked God to help me stop. But it's not working. I do it more than ever.
—Andrew

What's the big deal with looking at pictures in Playboy? *My dad did it when he was my age. And so did my grandpa. And they turned out okay.*
—Corey

Evan was supposed to have the house all to himself. That was the plan. His parents were visiting his sister at college. And for the first time in the history of the Ducane family, Evan didn't have to go with them.

That meant he was looking at about 10 hours of quality alone time. And he knew how he was going to spend two of them. He pulled a DVD from his backpack. *The Ever-Present Threat: Political Unrest in Nicaragua.* Evan grinned as he looked at the cover again.

When McPherson loaned him the DVD, he said no one would ever open a case with that title on it. No one except him and Evan, that is. Because they were the only ones who knew what was inside.

Evan opened the case and double-checked the title on the disc. *Girls Will Be Girls—The Unrated Version.* He put the disc in and hit "Play" on the remote control. He started to stretch out on the couch.

Before he got comfortable, though, he sat up and looked around to make sure he hadn't overlooked anything. The family room curtains were closed. No one could see in. The front door was locked, but not bolted. That made him a little nervous. The back door was probably locked. But no one ever used it anyway, so he wasn't worried about it.

As the movie's opening credits rolled, Evan decided it was better to be safe than sorry. He got up, walked to the front door, and slid the dead bolt into place. While he was up, he figured it would be a good idea to make himself comfortable. So he dashed upstairs to his room and put on some old sweatpants. Then he headed back downstairs to where the girls who will be girls were waiting for him.

Before he returned to the couch, he decided he needed one more thing—a cold can of root beer. As he passed through the family room on his way to the kitchen, he was careful not to look at the TV screen. He didn't want to spoil his viewing experience. But judging from the sounds of it, the girls were already busy being girls.

As he turned the corner into the dining room, Evan jumped back in surprise and let out a startled gasp. His grandparents were standing in the kitchen!

"Grandma, Grandpa, what are you doing here?" he asked in a shaky voice.

"We didn't mean to scare you, honey," his grandma said. "Your mom asked us to look in on you. We tried our key in the front door, but the dead bolt was locked. We thought you might be sleeping in, so we didn't ring the bell. Luckily the back door was unlocked."

Evan made a mental note to check and recheck the back door lock next time.

"What's that noise?" his grandpa asked as he started toward the family room. "It sounds like...grunting."

Evan's eyes grew wide, and his heart started to pound like a jackhammer in his chest. "I was, um, watching...tennis...on ESPN," he said.

"Oh, really, who's playing?" his grandpa asked. He seemed interested in watching.

"Uh...it's a couple of foreign players I've never heard of," Evan replied.

Just as his grandpa was about to turn the corner into the family room, his grandma spoke up. "Ray, we didn't come here so you could sit on a couch all day and watch sports with your grandson. Now put these tomatoes in the refrigerator."

Evan breathed a silent sigh of relief and slipped quietly out of the kitchen. He made a mad dash to the family room, grabbed the remote control with shaky hands, and finally managed to hit the stop button on his third try.

Just as his grandparents walked into the room.

After a few minutes of grandparentish chit-chat, Evan had the house to himself again. He collapsed on the couch and started thinking about "What if?" What if his grandparents had walked in 10 minutes later? What if they'd seen what was really on the screen? What if they'd found him sprawled on the couch...

Evan shuddered at the thought. It was too humiliating to imagine.

You'd think that would have been a wake-up call for Evan, but it wasn't. Two days later his mom almost caught him watching *Girls Will Be Girls* on his desktop computer.

Evan knows what will happen if he gets caught with porn, and he's scared to death of the consequences. But he just can't stop himself. The thrill is too addictive.

And he's not alone.

No One's Immune

R&B singer R. Kelly was accused of having sex with underage girls. Prosecutors claim to have videotapes made by the singer himself. Kelly was one of the biggest stars in music when the scandal hit. If the charges are true, that means he was willing to risk his fame, fortune, career, reputation—even his future—for a few minutes of illegal thrills.

Basketball star Kobe Bryant was accused of having nonconsensual sex with a woman in a Colorado hotel room. Bryant is considered the brightest star in the NBA. Advertisers line up to have him endorse their products. He has a beautiful wife and a supportive family. And if the charges are true, he was willing to throw all of that out the window for an opportunity to satisfy himself. At the critical moment, nothing else mattered to him but his sexual lust.

Michael Jackson was once the biggest star in the entertainment universe. People loved his music, respected his talent, and laughed off his little quirks. But then those quirks started to get weirder. Rumors started to spread that maybe he liked kids a little too much. He was charged with child molestation, but the case was settled out of court. You'd think that brush with humiliation would have been a wake-up call, but it wasn't. Jackson later admitted in a nationally televised interview that he shared his bed with young boys. Months later he was charged yet again with child molestation—another case of someone risking so much because he couldn't control his desires.

[NOTE: As this book is being written, none of these celebrities have been convicted of their charges. My point is not to say these men are guilty, but to show that their inability to control their sexual compulsions put them in publicly humiliating situations.]

How about you? Have you ever been caught in a humiliating sexual situation? Not necessarily something illegal but definitely something embarrassing. Have you ever had any close calls? Has your mom ever asked you why you take so long in the shower? Have you ever worried someone will find out what you do in secret?

If so, how did it affect you? Did it make you want to change the things you do? Or did it just make you more careful not to get caught?

It's easy to step into the trap of sexual lust. Getting out is another matter. The jaws of the trap are strong. Its teeth are sharp and long. In this chapter we're going to talk about why sexual lust seems escape proof.

Turbocharged Lust

Some people may try to tell you that becoming a Christian or going to church every Sunday will make your sexual compulsions go away. Unfortunately that's not always the case. In fact, a church environment often makes the problem worse.

Think about the adrenaline rush that comes from giving in to a sexual compulsion. Now consider this: two of the major ingredients of that rush are secrecy and risk. Have you ever seen a movie where someone commits the "perfect crime" and gets away with it? That's the thrill of secrecy. The idea of doing something no one else knows about is a real rush. Maybe you can't "fool all the people all the time," as the old saying goes. But for many of us, it's tempting to try.

What really kicks up the intensity level of sexual compulsion is the risk of being discovered. For guys, danger is a like an adrenaline turbocharger. The possibility of getting caught is what gives a sexual compulsion its edge. If there were no danger in it, it would be just another bad habit instead of an irresistible itch.

That's why a church environment and sexual compulsion make for a combustible combination. Church people tend to consider sexual sins to be the worst of all vices. So if a guy in church is wrestling with sexual compulsion, he'll want to keep it a secret at all costs. He'd rather deal with the situation alone than risk being condemned and rejected—and he'll get a thrill from doing it.

If you're in a church—or a youth group or a Sunday school class or a Bible study or whatever—people expect you to act a certain way. And the consequences of being caught doing something sexual are a lot more severe than for a guy who doesn't go to church. The higher the consequences, the greater the danger. The greater the danger, the bigger the thrill.

That's why sexual sins carry such strong addictive power for churchgoing guys. And that's why there are countless guys attending church every week who live with the fear that they'll be discovered.

So Strong Yet So Weak

God gives us an example in his Word of what can happen when sexual lust runs amok. It's the story of Samson. If you know anything about Samson, you know he was strong—freakishly strong. This was a guy who single-handedly killed a thousand enemy Philistines using only a donkey's jawbone.

Samson had the kind of physical strength that only comes from God himself. He was "set apart to God" from the day he was born (Judges 13:5). God had a purpose for Samson's life that he wanted people to know about. That's why Samson never cut his hair. His long, flowing locks reminded people of his uncut commitment to God.

Any way you look at it, Samson had a sweet life. He was big. He was bad (in a good way). He was famous. And he had a tight relationship with God.

But Samson also had a weakness. He liked taboo sex. Check out his first words in the Bible: "I have seen a Philistine woman in Timnah; now get her for me as my wife" (Judges 14:2). As I mentioned earlier, the Philistines were the enemies of Samson's people. Samson could have had his pick from any of the godly young women of Israel. But he didn't want them. He wanted nastier thrills. He wanted forbidden fruit.

If satisfying his urges meant turning his back on God and his family, Samson was willing to do it. As strong as he was, he couldn't break the grip of his sexual compulsion.

Samson's marriage to the Philistine woman was cut short by her death. But that didn't end his sexual compulsion. Years later he became involved with another Philistine woman named Delilah.

Once his compulsions kicked in, Samson didn't stop until he got what he wanted. And in the process, he ended up losing everything: his position as a leader of Israel; his reputation as a man of God; his hair, the symbol of his commitment to God; and his incredible strength. His Philistine enemies captured him, and his eyes were gouged out. In the end, he died among the Philistines.

As tragic as Samson's story is, it does have a silver lining (for us, at least). If we can learn from the mistakes Samson made, we can avoid the kind of spectacular flameout that brought him down. The first step in becoming stronger than Samson is recognizing how his sexual obsession got started and how it grew beyond his control. Let's break it down into four steps.

Step 1: Getting Preoccupied

The Bible doesn't tell us exactly what Samson was thinking about between the time his wife died and the time he hooked up with Delilah, but it's probably safe to say that thoughts of forbidden women were never far from his mind. You can imagine the kind of dreams and fantasies he had.

Eventually he traveled to Gaza in the Philistine's land. Maybe he told himself there was no harm in just looking, even as he was making his way to the red-light district in town. Getting an eyeful of the Philistine prostitutes undoubtedly fired his fantasies even more.

Samson probably told himself the same things we tell ourselves about our sexual urges:

- "There's no harm in looking."
- "I'm not hurting anyone."
- "I can stop anytime I want."

The fact is, though, our thoughts are seeds that fertilize and grow into actions. And once they start growing, it's tough to kill them.

Step 2: Developing Rituals

Rituals are the things we do before we act on our compulsions. When something excites us, we do it over and over again. We make It a ritual.

Samson's rituals may have involved making return trips to Gaza or flirting with prostitutes—something to get him close to the action to help him feel the rush of sexual thrill. He could have argued that technically he wasn't doing anything wrong. But he was inching closer to the line. Just like all guys do who start rituals for their sexual compulsions.

Do you have any rituals? Perhaps channel surfing late at night. Or browsing through men's magazines. Or entering certain words in your computer's search engine. It's easy to convince yourself that your rituals are harmless. But the fact is, once you start a ritual, you *will* ultimately act on your sexual compulsion. It's certain.

Step 3: Acting Out

Finally, during one of his trips Samson stepped over the line. He had sex with a Philistine prostitute (Judges 16:1). After resisting the urge for so long—after playing around with the idea again and again—Samson finally gave in. He opened the door for his lust and let it run wild.

He ignored his parents' wishes. He ignored his reputation as a spiritual leader. He ignored his relationship with God. With his lust running high, none of those things meant more to him than his sexual compulsion. So he made his choice.

Step 4: Feeling Guilty

Judges 16:3 gives us a clue about Samson's state of mind after his walk on the wild side. Apparently he'd entered the prostitute's house boldly. A few hours later, he left under the cover of darkness, hoping nobody would see him.

Does that seem like guilt to you? Whatever pleasure he enjoyed was washed away by remorse. But no matter how fast or how far he ran, Samson couldn't escape his guilty conscience.

Repeat Performance

After his first experience with the prostitute, Samson probably vowed to stay away from Gaza. Maybe you've made a similar vow after doing something you're ashamed of. But when boredom or stress returns, so does the desire for off-limits sex.

That's certainly what happened to Samson. After crossing the line once, the second time was easier. Much easier. In fact, his sexual cravings were probably stronger than before. That's why he went back to Gaza for more cheap thrills. And that's why his story has such a sad ending.

Every time you give in to your sexual compulsion—

- your sexual urges get more intense,
- your craving for risk increases, and
- your desire to resist the compulsion gets weaker.

Like a deadly whirlpool that pulls its victims under, sexual compulsion can drag down even the strongest guy. Just ask Samson.

That's the bad news. Here's the good news:

Freedom!

"For sin shall not be your master, because you are not under law, but under grace." That's a written guarantee from God for everyone who trusts Christ as Savior. You can look it up in Romans 6:14.

That wasn't always the case. Verses like Romans 5:21 and Galatians 3:22 make it clear that before we came to Christ, we were prisoners of sin. We were trapped by it. We had no choice but to obey our sinful impulses.

But then came Jesus. His life, death, and resurrection broke sin's stranglehold on us and changed our position. We're no longer slaves to sin; we've been set free. We don't *have* to obey our sinful impulses anymore; instead we have a choice. Romans 6:2 says that we have died to sin. That's permanent.

But don't start your victory dance just yet. As you've probably noticed, sin hasn't disappeared from the scene. It's no longer your master, but it's still your enemy. And you'll struggle with it every day of your life.

But it's a fight you can win.

You're not a slave to sin anymore. So don't act like one. "Therefore do not let sin reign in your mortal body so that you obey its evil desires." Those are Paul's instructions in Romans 6:12.

Jesus is your Master now. "In the same way, count yourselves dead to sin but alive to God in Christ Jesus" (Romans 6:11).

Want to know how to do that? Keep reading...

Getting Personal

1. When was the last time you felt trapped by sexual compulsion? What happened?

2. How do you think people at church would react if they knew about the sexual compulsions you struggle with?

3. How does it feel to know you're no longer a slave to sin? How will that affect your struggle against sexual compulsions?

CHAPTER FIVE

RAISING THE WHITE FLAG

Every time I try to stop, I go crazy. And I drive my family and friends crazy. It's not worth it.
—Danny

What I do when I'm alone is my business—and nobody else's.
—Chad

I had a big scare last night when my dad said he needed to use my computer. I was afraid he was gonna find my collection. I guess I should probably think about getting rid of it before I get caught.
—Brady

Josh picked up his desk calendar and threw it across the room. January 1. The first day of the year wasn't even over yet, and his New Year's resolution was shot. It was a familiar feeling. He'd made the same resolution a year earlier—and the year before that, too.

I will stop looking for things to masturbate to.

Josh laughed. Fifteen hours earlier, that had actually seemed doable. But that was before he stumbled across the *Sports Illustrated* swimsuit edition he'd hidden in his bookcase two years earlier.

The moment he saw the blonde in a thong on the cover, Josh knew what he was going to do. He couldn't stop himself. And he didn't even try.

When it was over, Josh put the magazine in his nightstand drawer—where he wouldn't forget it again. *I've already blown my New Year's resolution,* he told himself. *So there's no reason to stop now.*

Does Josh's story seem at all familiar to you? Have you ever tried to stop masturbating to erotic images? Do you ever worry that your self-pleasuring habit is turning into an addiction?

Nay Say

Some people will tell you the war for control over your sexual urges can't be won. They'll tell you that a guy's sexual desires are just too powerful to be controlled. They'll tell you that trying to live God's way will have you walking around sexually frustrated and miserable all the time.

But that's quitter talk.

What do you do when your coach has you running your fifth set of ladder drills during a preseason workout? When your lungs feel like they're going to explode in your chest, when your leg muscles wobble like cooked spaghetti and threaten to collapse beneath you, and when the stitch in your side feels like a knife in your ribs?

Do you just stop running and walk away from the workout? Do you tell yourself you're not tough enough to handle your coach's demands?

Not if you're serious about playing.

Instead you reach down for that last burst of energy. You grit your teeth. You ignore the pain in your legs and side. And you blow past the guys on either side of you for a big finish that gets your coach's attention. And at the end of the workout, you go home with the confidence that you can handle anything your coach throws at you.

What do you do when your honors calculus class starts to kick your academic butt? When you discover the material is a lot harder than you thought it would be? When the teacher turns out to be a lot less lenient—and a lot more boring—than you expected? When the homework starts eating up most of your evening hours? When your GPA hangs in the balance?

Do you drop the class like a hot potato? Do you replace it with a blow-off elective? A class that offers a guaranteed A with minimum effort on your part?

Not if you're serious about your education—not to mention your college future.

Instead you buckle down. You figure out what the problem

is, and you take care of it. You ask for extra assistance from your teacher. You get a tutor. You bust your tail to understand the test material. You eat, sleep, and breathe calculus until it becomes second nature to you. And you finish the class in style, with the confidence that no subject is too tough for you.

That's the mindset of a winner.

Fighting the Good Fight

What do you do when you realize your sexual compulsions are starting to overrun your life? When you spend hours in front of the computer or TV looking for things to masturbate to, or when you can't have a conversation with a girl without fantasizing about her?

Do you let it happen without a fight? Do you stop worrying about what's right and wrong? Do you convince yourself that your sex drive is just too strong to control?

Not if you're serious about offering your body as a living sacrifice to God.

Instead you put on your game face. You shift into warrior mode. You stop treating your compulsion like a friend and start treating it like the enemy it is.

Obviously, that's easier said than done. One guy described his own struggle this way: "I don't understand myself at all, for I really want to do what is right, but I don't do it. Instead I do the very thing I hate...But I can't help myself because it is sin inside me that makes me do these evil things."

Sounds like a typical guy, doesn't he? A regular fellow being pelted on all sides by temptation. An average Joe whose sinful nature is always threatening to bust out in a big way. A guy who knows firsthand what kind of damage compulsion can do.

Would it surprise you to learn that those words came from the apostle Paul? (You can read his surprising admission in Romans 7:15, 17.) Think about that. This was a guy chosen by God himself to help start the first churches, to spread the word about Jesus to people who knew nothing about him. This was the guy who wrote most of the New Testament, for crying out loud!

And he wrestled with the same feelings of guilt, self-loathing, and helplessness you and I wrestle with. If a guy like Paul struggled with those things, it's probably safe to say that no guy is immune to them.

Don't misunderstand Paul's words, though. Yes, sometimes he became frustrated by the power of his enemy, but he wasn't a quitter. He refused to give up the fight. Every time his sin knocked him down, he got back up for another round.

Are you ready to go the distance in fighting your sexual compulsions?

Scouting Report

Before you step into the ring, you need to size up your enemy. How big of a problem have your sexual compulsions become? If you're not going to be brutally honest, don't bother answering the question because it won't do you any good. If you've got a serious problem, you need to admit it.

If you're not sure how serious your problem is, here are four questions to help you figure it out.

1. Is your behavior a secret?

Are you doing things you refuse to tell others about? If the people closest to you knew what you're doing, would it change their feelings about you? Are you telling lies to cover your behavior? If so, you're isolating yourself from your loved ones. And you're starting a relationship with a habit that could become addictive.

2. Is your behavior abusive?

Does your sexual behavior create emotional (or physical) pain for you or others? Is it degrading? Does it exploit other people—say, for instance, women in magazines? Do you get pleasure from watching other people being abused in some way?

If you answered "yes" to any of these questions, you need to take your behavioral pulse. (Wouldn't you worry if you saw this behavior in someone else?)

3. Is your behavior used to deaden painful feelings?

Do you ever use masturbation to change your mood? Do you masturbate (or search for some other sexual outlet) when you're depressed? How about when you're bored? Or when you're angry?

Using masturbation to erase pain in your life is an addictive behavior.

4. Is your behavior a substitute for genuine commitment and caring?

Do you ever use masturbation to get the kind of intimacy that's missing in your personal relationships?

If you answered yes to any one of the previous four questions you've got a major fight going on in your life.

The Moment of Truth

If you've reached the point where you're ready to do something about your sexual compulsion, chances are you have a good reason. For better or worse, most guys don't face their compulsions until they're forced to. Something happens that compels them to admit their life is out of control.

So what's your story? What brings you to this point? Did you—

- Accidentally leave a porno disc in the family DVD player?
- Run up a major phone bill calling 1-900 sex lines?
- Forget to trash some X-rated photos you downloaded?
- Get busted shoplifting a *Playboy*?

Remember Samson? His moment of truth came near the end of his life. Blinded by his lust, he slept in Delilah's lap while a Philistine barber cut off his hair, which happened to be the source of his incredible strength.

As soon as the last clump of hair hit the floor, the Philistines rushed in and did what they'd wanted to do since they first laid eyes on the big guy: they overpowered him. Separated from God's strength, Samson was powerless to resist. And that's when things turned ugly.

His enemies gouged out his eyes and turned him into a freak-show attraction. They gave the Philistine people a chance to mock and laugh at the champion who had terrorized them for so long.

But a funny thing happened on the way to Samson's ultimate humiliation. His hair began to grow again. And so did his relationship with God. The Lord forgave Samson and used him one last time. The hero of the Israelites pulled down a Philistine temple, destroying himself and his enemies.

Samson learned firsthand what every guy must know. God is the God of second chances. And third chances. And fourth chances. He never gives up on us.

But before we can experience God's amazing grace, we have to admit we need it. We have to turn to him for help. Many times we have to turn to other people for help, too. And that's not an easy thing to do. Because if you're like most guys, your first instinct is to say, "I can handle the problem myself."

And that's a mistake. You see, you can't rely on your own endurance or strength to win the battle against your compulsions.

You Can't Overpower Your Lust

Remember the apostle Paul's words in Romans 7? The stuff about doing things he didn't want to do and not doing things he wanted to do? If a guy like Paul couldn't overpower his compulsive sin by himself, it would be pretty arrogant for us to think we can. Especially when our entire culture seems geared to keeping sex on our brains 24-7.

Here's a for instance. Let's say tomorrow morning you decide to try to make it through the entire day without once lusting after a female. Think about the erotic minefield you'd have to make your way through: the bikini-wearing girl on the billboard on the way to school, the hot substitute teacher you can't keep your eyes off of; the guy next to you in English lit. who wants to tell you how far he got with one of the cheerleaders, the magazine rack at the convenience store, the half-naked female characters on your favorite TV shows—plus the hundreds of other sexual temptations that will be screaming for your attention throughout the day.

You don't have to go looking for sexual temptation; it's everywhere. That's why you can't control your lust by yourself. You're hopelessly outnumbered on your own.

I remember a friend once told me with a straight face, "I'll never have a problem with sexual lust."

I looked at him and said, "You're absolutely amazing. If that's true, you're stronger than Samson, godlier than David, and wiser than Solomon."

He sat down and stared at me for a half minute without uttering a word. And then he said, "I never thought of it like that."

I'll guarantee you that if Samson, David, and Solomon were here, they'd all say, "You can't defeat your lust alone!"

You Can't Reform Your Lust

Okay, you may be thinking, *maybe I can't overpower my lust. But I can make myself better. I can reform my lust. After all, I'm a Christian. I read the Bible. And I pray.*

Unfortunately, our appetite for lust is so evil that it will use even God's commands to tempt us. Check out what Paul says: "I found that the very commandment that was intended to bring life actually brought death. For sin, seizing the opportunity afforded by the commandment, deceived me, and through the commandment put me to death" (Romans 7:10-11).

God's law excites our lust: We want what we can't have. The more forbidden something seems, the more it appeals to us. God says no, and our lust says yes, yes, yes. God says *do,* and our lust says *don't.*

Trying to reform our lust is like trying to turn a dog into a person. For 13 years our family owned a cocker spaniel named Pumpkin. During those years I taught Pumpkin all kinds of tricks—not just the everyday stuff like sit, lie down, and roll over. I also trained her to jump through a hoop, close a door, sit on her hind legs, and fall over dead when I shot her with an imaginary gun.

Yet in spite of all my training, I couldn't keep Pumpkin from acting like a dog. She always did doggy things. She ate things people hate to get on their shoes. She sniffed other dogs in places only dogs sniff. She went to the bathroom in public. No matter how well I trained Pumpkin, she was still a dog.

In the same way, your tendency to sin doesn't change when you come to faith in Christ. You can go to church, read your Bible, pray every day, and even become a student leader in your youth group—all without reforming your sinful nature.

And when your sinful nature dominates, you're capable of doing anything evil—whether you're a believer or not. When lust takes control, your odds of reforming it are about as good as those of a dog reciting the lyrics to "Stairway to Heaven."

You Can't Starve Your Lust

The natural tendency in dealing with an addiction or compulsion is just to quit cold turkey. But that's not enough. Abstinence alone won't kill your lust. Don't get me wrong; that's a great start. But if your only strategy is to stop masturbating, you won't solve your problem with sexual compulsion. You'll just find another way to act it out.

The brutal truth is, until the day you come face to face with the Lord, you'll wrestle with sin. Several years ago I read a poem by Shel Silverstein called "The Yipiyuk," which describes the struggle and defeat that comes from trying to fight alone against an enemy like lust.

In the swamplands long ago,
Where the weeds and mudglumps grow,
A Yipiyuk bit on my toe...
Exactly why I do not know.
I kicked and cried
And hollered "Oh"—
The Yipiyuk would not let go.
I whispered to him soft and low—
The Yipiyuk would not let go.
I shouted "Stop," "Desist" and "Whoa"—
The Yipiyuk would not let go.
Yes, that was sixteen years ago,
And the Yipiyuk still won't let go.
The snow may fall,
The winds may blow—
The Yipiyuk will not let go.
The snow may melt,
The grass may grow—
The Yipiyuk will not let go.

I drag him 'round each place I go.
This Yipiyuk that won't let go.
And now my child at last you know
Exactly why I walk so slow.

Like the Yipiyuk, your sinful nature will hold on tight. You may be able to ignore it for a while. You may try to convince yourself and others that it doesn't really have a hold on you. But if you want to break its power, you must first realize it's there and admit you don't have the power to shake it loose.

The sooner you get tired of fighting a losing battle against lust, the better. Look at Paul's words of desperation when he got tired of fighting: "What a wretched man I am! Who will rescue me from this body of death?" (Romans 7:24).

That's not quitter talk. It's the talk of someone who's tired of kidding himself with macho bluster. It's the talk of someone who realizes he needs reinforcements to fight the battle ahead. It's the talk of someone who understands he has to take his fight to the next level. It's the talk of someone who's ready to call in the big guns.

It's the talk of someone who's serious about defeating his lust.

Have you reached the point where you realize you can't defeat your lust by yourself? Are you ready to call God into the fight? If so, then you're ready to take your next step toward freedom.

Read on.

Getting Personal

1. Do you think your masturbation habit has gotten out of control? If so, what are some signs that it's out of control? If not, what makes you think you have it under control?

2. What are the top 10 things that are most likely to ruin your efforts to overpower your lust by yourself? Be specific. Think of the TV shows, daily situations, people, and anything else that tends to fire up your lust.

3. What's your biggest concern when it comes to admitting you need help dealing with your lust?

CHAPTER SIX

DRAGGING IT INTO THE LIGHT

I've done some things that even God can't forgive.
—Kenny

Why can't people mind their own business about the stuff that happened to me when I was a kid? It's in the past, and that's where it's going to stay.
—Marcellus

I may have some problems with self-control. But at least I'm not as bad as some guys I know.
—Matt

I was speaking to a large group of high school students in Northern California when I realized something wasn't quite right. As I spoke, I noticed the group was laughing at inappropriate times. I usually use a lot of humor in my talks, so at first I assumed the group was just a little slow on the draw. That maybe my jokes were hitting home a few seconds late.

But the inappropriate laughter continued. So I did what any guy would do in that situation. I nonchalantly tried to check my fly. But then I realized I couldn't do it without everyone seeing. So I just held my Bible in front of the barn door for the rest of my talk and tried to make it look casual.

When I finished speaking, I was surprised to discover that my pants were zipped. Several students gathered around me and began asking questions. Before I answered them, I had one of my own: "Why were you all laughing throughout my talk?"

"Oh," said one of the girls with a giggle, "because of your Texas accent."

Randy (the other author of this book) once went trolling for porn with his parents—without even realizing what he was doing. It happened several years ago, at the beginning of the Internet age. His parents had just gotten their first computer, complete with Internet hookup. Randy, being a dutiful son, was showing them how to use their search engine.

It just so happened that a Barenaked Ladies song was playing on the radio at the time. So Randy typed in the words "Barenaked Ladies" just to get some info about the band. (So don't get any weird ideas.)

As you can probably guess, the sites that came up had very little to do with the Canadian rock band and a lot to do with sex. All kinds of sex. The kind of sex you don't want to see on a computer screen with your parents looking over your shoulder.

And did I mention that Randy's father is a Baptist minister?

You could probably share some embarrassing stories of your own. Unfortunately, nobody gets out of this world without being embarrassed at one time or another. Some guys seem to make a career out of embarrassment. They know what it's like to be laughed at or whispered about, and they're not particularly concerned about it.

Most of us, though, would rather go one-on-one with a rabid pit bull than endure an embarrassing situation. The idea of other people seeing us when we're vulnerable or knowing we've done something stupid or humiliating is enough to make our skin crawl.

Toxic Shame

Believe it or not, the shame that comes from being embarrassed is healthy. It reminds you you're human and keeps you from taking yourself too seriously. But there's another kind of shame that's not healthy. In fact, it's toxic. It's like radioactive waste that destroys its container. It eats away at you from the inside. And if you don't take care of it, it can do serious damage.

That kind of shame has to do with who you are as a guy. It comes from believing that you've failed yourself—and, even worse, that you've failed God. Typically a guy who struggles with this type of shame—

- sees himself as someone who can't be trusted,
- tries to prevent other people from getting too close, and

- is afraid to look too closely at himself, for fear of what he might see.

As a result he feels alienated from God. He feels alienated from his friends and loved ones. He even feels alienated from himself.

With all of that alienation, he needs to feel intimate with someone—or something—safe. So he latches on to a sexual habit or experience. Maybe it's pornography. Or compulsive masturbation. Or something really kinky. All that matters to him is that it feels like intimacy—even though it's actually anything but intimacy.

The problem is, every time he goes looking for that kind of false intimacy, he comes away with more shame. And the more shame he experiences, the more he needs to deaden his feelings—with the false intimacy that's causing his shame. And on and on it goes. A vicious cycle.

Shamefaced

The thing is, most guys prefer that vicious cycle to the alternative: facing their shame. That's a tall order for any guy.

There's nothing new about wanting to avoid shame. People have been doing it since—well, just about the beginning of human history.

Look again at the story of Adam and Eve in the Garden of Eden. Genesis 2:25 tells us they "were both naked, and they felt no shame." That must've been incredible—having nothing to hide and being completely intimate with each other and with God.

And then sin entered the picture. Because they disobeyed God, Adam and Eve experienced guilt for the first time. They became spiritually scarred.

Notice what their first reaction was—fear. They were afraid God would see their sin and reject them. So they hid. They tried to cover their shame. Just like we do.

But God wasn't in the mood for hide-and-seek. He dragged Adam and Eve out of hiding. He dragged their sin into the light. He exposed what they had tried to keep to themselves. He didn't do it to humiliate them. He did it because it was the only way to rebuild intimacy with him—and with each other.

Dodgeball

If you're serious about having a tight relationship with God, you need to drag your shame into the light. In order to do that, you have to stop avoiding the truth about yourself.

When was the last time you played dodgeball? As a kid I loved the game. I was quick enough to avoid most balls that were thrown my way. And if I couldn't avoid one, I'd catch it and throw it at an opponent. And he'd be out.

I think a lot of guys have become experts at spiritual dodgeball. We've learned to avoid responsibility for the things we do. And when the truth come a little too close to us, we throw it at someone (or something) else.

But now's the time to stop playing. Instead of dodging the truth, try embracing it. That's right, *embrace* it. Face every one of those nasty secrets about yourself and your family. Secrets about—

- physical or sexual abuse,
- alcoholism or brutal family fights,
- drug use,
- imperfections you never talk about, and
- your own sexual behavior.

Those secrets are the real source of your shame. They're the reason you believe no one would love you if they really knew you. They're the reason you keep other people—even your closest friends—at an arm's distance.

Taking Responsibility

You have to understand, though, that your painful secrets aren't excuses. You can't use them to justify your behavior. They are what they are—the difficult truth about your past and present.

Once you've faced your secrets, you have to think about the people you've been playing spiritual dodge ball with. The ones you've tried to throw blame to. You need to admit to yourself that no one else is to blame for your sexual predicament. Not your parents. Not the girls at school who like to show off their bods. Not the geeks who create porn sites.

You are responsible for your own sexual behavior. That's the painful truth.

If you're ready to deal with that truth, here's what I want you to do. Write out three lists.

On the first list write down every shameful secret about yourself that you can think of.

On the second list write down every excuse you've used to explain your behavior.

On the third list write down the names of everyone you've ever blamed for your problems.

Once you've made the lists, you're ready for the next step.

Taking It to God

Once you've dealt with the truth about your problems, you need to share it with God. At first that may seem like a scary thing to do. But you can take a little comfort in the fact that he already knows everything about it anyway.

You can take even more comfort from the story of the prodigal son in Luke 15:11-32. If you're not familiar with the story, I'll give you the highlights. A young man looking for some action and excitement demands his inheritance from his father. He makes it clear that he cares more about his father's money than about his father.

The father reluctantly agrees to give him the money. And the young man hits the road with a pocketful of spending cash. His journey takes him to a distant country, where he proceeds to party his brains out like every day is spring break—with all the friends, women, and booze money can buy.

No party lasts forever, of course. In time the young man's money runs out—followed closely by his "friends" and women. Strapped for cash, he takes a job feeding pigs. He's lonely, he's miserable, and he's hungry. When the pig food starts to look good to him, he realizes he's bottomed out. So he comes to his senses and realizes there's only one place to go.

Filled with shame, he returns home. On the way he rehearses what he'll say to his father to make things right. He reviews every sin he's committed against the old man. He searches for the right way to say, "I screwed up big-time, and I need your forgiveness and help."

The prodigal son was at the same point in his life that you may be in yours. And perhaps like you, he wasn't sure how his father would respond. But what the prodigal son discovered about his father is what I hope you'll learn about God.

Understanding God's Love

No matter how disgusting your life has become, you're never too dirty for your heavenly Father to love. In fact, do you know what he's doing right now? He's waiting for you to come to him.

Look at the way the prodigal son's father reacted when he saw his boy. He didn't wait for the kid to come groveling. The father ran to meet him. He embraced him. He kissed him. He made his son feel loved and wanted—regardless of what he'd done.

That's how God feels about you. Even if you've turned your back on him. Even if you've done some seriously twisted things. Even if you don't believe anyone could ever love you.

Not only does God love you; he accepts you. And he's ready to use you in his plan. That's right, *you.* He has important work for you to do—no matter how bad your past is.

Accepting Yourself as God Does

Don't get me wrong. This isn't a TV sitcom where all problems vanish in a half hour. I'm not telling you that your shame will disappear completely the moment you mention it to God. No matter how strong your bond is to him, you'll still occasionally struggle with the fear of being rejected. And when your lust causes you to start up an old habit, you'll have to deal with your anti-self feelings ("I'm so pathetic—I don't deserve forgiveness") all over again.

That's when it's important to remind yourself where those thoughts are really coming from. They're not coming from you. They're coming from your sinful nature, courtesy of Satan. Remember, he'll use any tactic to pull you away from God. And if guilt and shame work on you, guess what he's going to keep using again and again and again.

Your best defense against his attacks is the truth. And the truth is, God loves you unconditionally. No matter what you've done or how many times you've done it. Remember, no one's standards are higher than God's. So if he says you're worth loving, you don't need a second opinion. You can love yourself.

That's something to keep in mind. Something to tell yourself—often. When you're alone, say something like this out loud: "God loves me unconditionally. I receive his love. And I love myself." If you've been telling yourself most of your life that you're a terrible person, it will probably take some time to change your opinion. So just keep trying.

Remember, there's nothing you can do to make yourself more lovable to God. I'll say it again: He loves you unconditionally. If you refuse to believe that, you're calling God a liar. You're saying you know your value better than he does.

And how dumb is that?

Getting Personal

1. How often do you struggle with feelings of shame? What kinds of things trigger those feelings?

2. How hard was it for you to write down your shameful secrets and excuses? What made it so difficult?

3. What makes you feel distant from God? What makes you feel closer to him?

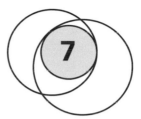

CHAPTER SEVEN

CHOOSING YOUR MASTER

I can quit masturbating any time I want. I just don't want to yet.
—Hyung

How many times does it usually take before a guy actually stops? 'Cause I've tried three times already. Is that bad?
—T.J.

What's the worst that could happen if I don't stop?
—Antoine

I'm a barefoot water-skier. I love the feeling of skimming across glass-smooth water at high speeds. I love the spray of water at my sides. And I love the challenge of performing tricks without skis.

Over the years many friends have asked me if I can teach them how to ski barefoot. I always answer the same way: "If you're willing to fall on your face while traveling 40 miles an hour again and again and again, I can teach you."

Almost all of them were up for the challenge. At least they said they were. They told me they were ready to give it a try, despite my warnings.

Once they were on the water, though, most of them gave up after a few face plants. As their confidence faded, so did their desire to ski barefoot. A few, however, absolutely refused to give up. They didn't care how many times they fell or how much pain they experienced. They were determined to ski barefoot. Or die trying.

What's the difference between those who gave up and those who kept trying? It's not intelligence. Or tolerance for pain. Or courage. Or athletic ability. I think the difference is commitment. Some guys made up their minds before they even stepped onto the water that they *would* ski barefoot. And eventually they did.

Other guys liked the *idea* of being able to ski barefoot. But when it turned out to be not so easy, they gave up. They didn't count the cost before they started, and that's always a bad idea. If you're going to succeed, you have to count the cost. And that is true whether you're water-skiing barefoot or defeating your sexual compulsions.

Hard Changes

If you're addicted to masturbation or porn or any other sexual habit, changing your lifestyle won't be easy. Even if you're not addicted—if you're just starting to explore your compulsion—you'll find it hard to get back to the sexual purity you had before.

Let's face it: choosing to be sexually pure means giving up something you enjoy. It means staring down the boredom and shame you're trying to escape. It means saying no to an intense craving for pleasure and enjoyment.

In other words, being sexually pure demands extreme commitment. And before you commit to something as serious as that, you owe it to yourself to count the cost. That way you can prepare yourself for the challenges that lie ahead. You can guard against being blindsided by emotions and difficulties you didn't anticipate.

A big part of counting the cost is taking a good look at the consequences of your sexual sin and the benefits of sexual purity. Many guys have found that seeing those consequences and benefits laid out for them has helped them strengthen their commitment to be pure.

Maybe it'll work for you, too. Try making a list of the negative things that can happen when you let your sexual compulsions control your actions. Your list should include consequences you've already suffered. Perhaps that includes a damaged relationship with your parents. Or trouble relating to real-life girls as opposed to the fantasy women of porn. Or feeling disgusted with yourself. Whatever it is, put it on your list.

If you're not a natural list maker, here's a tip for you. Think about worst-case scenarios. Imagine what might happen if your compulsion completely steamrolled over your life. Then write down what might happen in several different areas of your life. Here's a guide to help you.

Painful Consequences If I Continue

1. To my relationship with God:

2. To my girlfriend:

3. To my future wife:

4. To my health:

5. To my reputation:

6. To my close friends:

7. To my self-image:

8. To my future:

Once you've finished that list, start a second one. This time think about the flip side of the issue. Imagine what would happen if you stopped giving in to your sexual compulsion. For now I want you to focus on the negative things, the consequences that make it difficult to say no to your lust.

If you've ever tried unsuccessfully to quit looking at porn or masturbating compulsively, write down the things that kept you from reaching your goal.

Painful Consequences If I Stop

1. Boredom

2. Enduring emotional pain instead of trying to deaden it

3. Intense craving for former sexual experiences

4. _____

5. _____

Most guys who struggle with compulsive sexual behavior eventually reach a point of desperation. Usually, it happens when someone discovers your secret. Or when your guilt and shame get to be too much for you to deal with. God uses situations like those as wake-up calls.

For some guys, though, a simple wake-up call isn't enough. Sometimes God has to pound a guy over the head with a mallet in order to get his attention. And if that's what it takes, God will do it. He's that serious about sexual purity. So do yourself a favor. Open your eyes now.

If you can imagine all the pain and trouble your sexual compulsion is causing, you can start to see how much better it is to make a commitment to stay pure. No matter how difficult that may seem.

After you've finished your first two lists, I want you to make one more. This time I want you to think about the benefits of staying sexually pure.

Benefits of Purity

1. To my relationship with God:

2. To my girlfriend:

3. To my future wife:

4. To my health:

5. To my reputation:

6. To my close friends:

7. To my self-image:

8. To my future:

I want you to dig down deep as you make this list. Don't just settle for obvious answers. For example, you could make a difference in a friend's life by being an example to him. If he sees you winning the battle against lust, he's going to be impressed (though he probably won't tell you he's impressed). He's also going to be curious about where you got such strength. If he sees the difference God is making in your life, he may be interested in finding out what God can do in his life.

When you lay out all the benefits and consequences, you'll see that the logical choice is sexual purity. Unfortunately, we guys aren't always known for our logic—especially when lust is involved. We tend to do things that create all kinds of problems for ourselves, just for the sake of temporary pleasure.

I'm challenging you to resist the urge to be illogical. Take a good look at the cost of your sexual compulsions. Make a commitment to turn away from your sexual habits before they cause any more damage in your life.

One Good Turn Deserves Another

I should point out that turning *away* from sexual sin isn't the end of the process. You also have to turn *to* God. Think of it as a simultaneous action—like a trapeze artist who's about to jump. Not only is he committing to let go of the trapeze, but he's also committing to grab his partner's arms. Without both commitments, he'll fall. The same thing goes for you. If you don't let go of your sexual sin and turn to God, you'll fall, too.

Turning to God means taking the time to think through exactly what God wants you to do—and then deciding to do it, with God's help and by his grace.

When the apostle Paul urges us to present our bodies as living sacrifices to God, he calls it a "reasonable" thing to do (Romans 12:1, NKJV). So he's saying it's a logical move. In the previous 11 chapters of Romans, Paul reminds his readers that God's mercy has given us forgiveness, acceptance, freedom from lust, an awesome future, and the power to live a victorious life.

If he doesn't deserve your complete devotion after all that, who does? What has pornography—or masturbation—done to deserve your devotion? Absolutely nothing. Remember—anything that controls your life is taking what rightfully belongs to God. And he's not big on sharing what's his.

Why Not?

On paper it all seems so logical, doesn't it? After weighing the benefits and consequences, we might ask, "Why would anyone who's serious about pleasing God not make a commitment to him immediately?" It's a good question. Let's take a look at four common reasons that guys give for their lack of commitment. See if any of them seem familiar to you.

Reason #1: "I want to wait until I've straightened myself out."

At first that may seem like a noble way of thinking—wanting to make yourself acceptable before you give yourself to God. But that's like spending a day making your house spotless before the cleaning lady arrives. It doesn't make sense. God doesn't ask us to fix ourselves and then turn to him. He wants us to come to him broken so he can heal us.

God loves you just the way you are. *God's* power—not yours—is what you need in order to change. In John 15:1-8, Jesus compares our relationship with him to branches on a vine. We're the branches. The branch's job is to stay attached to the vine and to bear fruit. The vine's job is to produce the fruit.

Living a sexually pure life is a fruit of our relationship with God. He's the one who produces it. We're the ones who bear it. We can't do that without a relationship with him.

Reason #2: "I've committed myself to God before, and it didn't work."

Many guys believe that when they commit themselves to God, he removes their lustful desires the way a surgeon might remove a tumor. They expect to be lust-free for the rest of their lives. When they find out that's not the case, they get confused and discouraged. Sometimes they tell themselves the Lord didn't hold up his end of the bargain, and they go back to their old ways.

Don't make that mistake. You need to understand from the start that God doesn't take away your lust when you come to him. He's not in the business of doing your work for you. But he does give you the instructions and the power you need to control your lust.

Reason #3: "I committed myself to God a long time ago, so I don't need to do it again."

Have you ever heard of married couples "renewing" their wedding vows? Different couples do it for different reasons. Some do it to celebrate a major anniversary. Others do it as a way to reconnect after an affair or some other problem. They don't actually remarry each other because they're already married. They simply renew their commitment to one another. They revitalize their passion for their relationship.

Sometimes guys need to do the same thing with God. We need to renew our commitment. We need to officially tell God— and ourselves—that he is our Lord and Master. And we need to pursue sexual purity with a revitalized passion and will to win.

Reason #4: "I'm not worthy to commit myself to God."

Some guys feel unworthy of God's love. Perhaps it's because they can't control their sexual compulsions. And you know what? Their feelings are correct. Those guys are *not* worthy of God's love. Neither am I, and neither was—

- Jacob, who cheated his own brother out of his most

prized possession;
- Moses, who murdered a man in cold blood;
- Samson, whose sexual lust was as extreme as his strength;
- David, who cheated with a married woman and ordered her husband killed; or
- Peter, who denied his relationship with Jesus to save his own skin.

Here's a news flash for you: *no one* is worthy of God's love. Every one of us has choked in a major way.

Fortunately for us, God doesn't make us earn his favor. If he did, nothing short of perfection would be good enough. So we can all breathe a big sigh of relief that the Christian life isn't about being perfect. It's about taking a few steps, stumbling, getting back up, and taking a few more steps. With enough time and practice, we may learn not to stumble as often or fall as hard.

But one thing's for sure. No matter how pure we become, we'll never deserve God's favor. And we'll never be able to change ourselves. That's why it makes sense to devote yourself to the One who loves you no matter what and who has the power to change you.

Father and Son

Are you ready to take the leap? If you're convinced that committing yourself to God is the logical thing to do, why not do it now? Imagine yourself as a prodigal son returning home to your Father. You've done a lot of things you regret, a lot of things that have disappointed your Father.

But instead of holding a grudge against you, God is running to meet you with his arms wide open. Now's the time to tell him what you've done wrong. To tell him how sorry you are. And to tell him you're ready to serve him instead of your lust.

That's how you present your body as a living sacrifice. You give God your body. You live your life for him and allow him to live through you. That's how you get the strength to control your lust.

A Crisis of Faith

Once you dedicate yourself to God, two things will happen: First, God will help you see the areas of your life that need to be changed. It's true that he accepts you as you are. But he loves you too much to let you stay that way. So he'll show you the thoughts and actions that have to change if you're going to be sexually pure. He'll point out the things that can't be present in your life if you're going to be close to him.

But then a second thing will happen. As you start to think about the changes that need to be made, you'll experience a crisis of faith. The more serious you get about defeating your lust, the more you'll realize just how painful it's going to be—like hitting lake water face first at 40 miles an hour, time after time after time.

Your body will scream for you to satisfy your lust—just one more time. That's when you'll have to decide. Are you going to let God meet your needs, or are you going to try to meet them yourself? Will you obey God or not?

It's the same crisis people have been experiencing since biblical times. Whenever God calls someone, that person has to decide whether he believes God will take care of him. For Abraham that meant leaving his homeland and traveling to a foreign country. But he made the journey because he believed the Lord would protect him and meet his needs. Later he was ready to offer his son as a human sacrifice to God because he believed the Lord would raise him from the dead. (God stopped him from carrying out the sacrifice.) Whatever God asked, Abraham was ready to do.

That's the kind of extreme commitment God wants. He wants you to trust him to protect you and provide for you. He wants you to let him change the way you think and act.

You Can Do It!

Obviously, you're reading this book because you want to be pure. And that stirs the same emotions in me that I experienced when I was into barefoot waterskiing. I feel the same anticipation I felt when a friend and I would get up at sunrise and drive to the lake. After arriving we'd walk to the dock and climb into the boat. A two-foot layer of fog would hang over the surface of the water.

My friend's dream was to ski barefoot. Mine was to help him. I had done all I could to prepare him for that day. He was ready and committed. I knew he could do it.

I know you can accomplish your goal, too. And in the rest of this book, I'll show you how to how build on your commitment to God with a plan that will work.

Getting Personal

1. What's your biggest fear when you think about trying to overcome your sexual compulsions?

2. Before you started reading this book, if someone had asked you why you hadn't committed yourself to God, what would you have said?

3. What are three things you think God will point out that need to be changed in your life?

CHAPTER EIGHT

DISCOVERING THE NEW YOU

If I'm supposed to be a new person in Christ, why am I still doing the same old things? Why didn't he change me?
—Justin

If all my sins are already forgiven, it doesn't really matter how many times I masturbate—does it?
—Scott

If I keep doing the things I'm doing, does that mean I'm not really saved?
—Tracy

Remember the movie *13 Going on 30* with Jennifer Garner? Or *Big* with Tom Hanks? Or *All of Me* with Steve Martin? If you're a movie freak, you know that all three of these films have a common theme: transformation.

13 Going on 30 is the story of a young teenage girl who turns into a 30-year-old woman overnight. *Big* tells the story of a 13-year-old boy who makes a wish to be bigger and wakes up the next morning a grown man. *All of Me* shows how a man's life is transformed when the spirit of a dead woman invades his body.

If you're a true movie freak, you can probably name a dozen more films that feature characters who are changed from one thing to another. The idea of a person's life being completely transformed by a single event is a popular theme in Hollywood.

It's an even more popular theme in the New Testament. You can't swing a stick in the second half of the Bible without hitting a passage that talks about how followers of Jesus Christ are transformed.

The moment you made the decision to follow Christ, you became a new person. Something changed in your life. You may not be able to put your finger on it yet, but in time you'll recognize it. You'll begin to understand your new identity.

As I mentioned in chapter 7, once you devote yourself to Christ, God starts to point out areas in which you need to change. And no change is more important than your self-image, the way you think about who you are.

After you've dragged your shame into the light, confessed your sin, and devoted yourself to obeying the Lord, you're ready to take the next step. You're ready to begin allowing God to change the way you view yourself.

Unconditional Acceptance

The idea of someone accepting you unconditionally may be tough to comprehend, especially if you're used to people pointing out your faults. Or holding grudges against you. Or punishing you for past wrongs. You may wonder how God can overlook all the nasty things you've done. The truth is, he doesn't overlook them.

Remember *The Passion of the Christ?* Jesus suffered horribly and died on a cross in excruciating pain to pay for every wrong thing you've ever done. If that thought doesn't thrill and humble you at the same time, you need to keep thinking about it until it does.

When I first understood what Jesus had done and how it affected me, I let out a huge sigh of relief. I wasn't what you'd call a regular churchgoer as a young guy. And on the rare occasions I did go, I felt as out of place as a vegetarian at an all-you-can-eat steak house. I saw myself as a sinner and all the people around me as saints. I wondered what a person had to do to get on good terms with God.

My religious friends gave me all sorts of answers. Some told me I had to go to church. Others said I had to stop swearing. (You can imagine my response to that.) Still others said I had to be nice and stop treating girls like sex objects. No matter what the advice was, it all boiled down to the same thing: I had to earn God's favor with my actions.

I remember thinking, *If that's what it takes to have a relationship with God, I'm in serious trouble.* I couldn't stand church. I couldn't control my language. And I couldn't stop chasing girls.

When I found out the truth—that all I had to do was trust

Jesus to forgive me—I was seriously stoked because that was something I *could* do. I could believe that Jesus paid for my sins with his death. I could believe that his resurrection gives me eternal life. So one day I trusted Christ as my Savior.

And surprise, surprise! Things started changing immediately in my life. Habits I'd struggled with for years suddenly became no problem for me. I figured, *If it's that easy to become a new person, this Christianity thing should be a cinch.* And I started my new life, certain that my lust and vulgar language were problems of the past.

Four Steps to Freedom

Raise your hand if you think I had a rude awakening waiting for me. Okay, put your hand down. Of course I was wrong about my lust being a thing of the past. When it started to stir for the first time after I'd trusted Christ, I got scared. But I didn't panic. Instead I went looking for answers. And I found them in the writings of Paul.

Let me give you a breakdown of what I discovered. There are four steps to becoming free from lust's grip.

Step 1: Know who you are in Christ.

If someone asked you to describe yourself as a person, you could choose any number of answers. You could talk about your physical appearance ("I'm 5'11", 150 pounds, brown hair, brown eyes, scar above my right eyebrow."). You could mention your family history ("I'm an only child; my mom's a single mother; my parents were divorced when I was five."). You could describe your geographic background ("I was born in Indiana; I moved to Southern California when I was three; I've been living in

Minneapolis since I was in sixth grade."). Or you could list your likes and dislikes ("I'm a huge Cubs fan; I hate country music; I love anime."). All of those things say something about your identity.

But what if someone asked you to describe yourself as a Christian? Where would you start? What would you say about the way you live? About the things you're allowed to do? About the things that are off-limits to you?

Do you know who you are in Christ?

If you're not sure, you're not alone. Christians as far back as the first century have struggled with the idea of what it means to live for Christ. When Paul wrote his letter to the church in Rome, he knew some of the misunderstandings people were wrestling with—especially when it came to God's forgiveness.

Some people were claiming that if God forgives everyone who believes in Christ, we're free to do whatever we want—kind of like having unlimited credit at the Sin Store.

Paul pointed out that Christians who fall for that lie misunderstand their Christian identity. You see, as Christians, we've been identified with Christ in his death, burial, and resurrection: That's the foundation of our new identity.

Do you know what that means? It means everything that's true of Christ is true of us (except for the part about his being God). Paul described it this way: "I have been crucified with Christ and I no longer live, but Christ lives in me" (Galatians 2:20). The old Paul, everything he was before he met Jesus, died on the cross with Jesus. After meeting Jesus, Paul was new person.

If you want it spelled out more clearly, try 2 Corinthians 5:17:

"Therefore, if anyone is in Christ, he is a new creation; the old has gone, the new has come!"

Because we're new people, it makes no sense to live as we used to live. Christ gives us freedom from the power of sin and lust. Think about what having his power inside you means. Does sin have any power over Christ? Of course not. So that means sin has no power over you, either. Remember: What's true of Christ is true of you.

Several years ago I heard a story about a sailor who served under a harsh and demanding captain. After the sailor had washed the deck, the captain would make him wash it again. After the sailor had painted the railings, the captain would make him add another coat.

Finally the young sailor was discharged from the military. He no longer had to answer to the master who had controlled his every move.

Several weeks after his discharge, the ex-sailor ran into his old captain on the streets of a harbor town. When the captain saw him, he angrily ordered the young man back to the ship. The ex-sailor was so used to obeying the captain's orders that he immediately turned toward the wharf. Then he remembered he'd been released from the captain's authority. He no longer had to obey him or even listen to him. Instead of returning to the ship, he shook his head and walked away a free man.

That story illustrates what Paul says in Romans 6: You've been released from the power of lust. You have to understand that. You have the power of Christ in you. And nothing is stronger than that.

The risen Lord of the universe now lives in you. That's who

you are in Christ.

Step 2: Believe you live with Christ.

If lust has been smacking you around for a while, you may not feel as though its power has been broken in your life. You may not feel like a new person. If that's the case, don't trust your feelings. Trust Christ. He's shattered the power of sin in your life. That's a stone-cold fact.

His unlimited power is yours to use. Your faith is what unleashes it. Think about how much faith you exercise every day without even knowing it. Every time you sit down, you express faith in the chair that holds you. Every time you drive (or ride in) a car on a two-lane highway, you have faith in the fact that the drivers of oncoming cars won't cross the yellow line. Every time you travel by plane, you put your faith in the pilot to get you to your destination safely.

Now imagine what you can accomplish if you harness your faith in Christ and use it like a weapon in your fight against sexual lust. Keep in mind that Christ's power over sin won't do you any good unless you use it. You do that by believing that all that's true of him is true of you and by trusting him to live his life through you.

Step 3: Give yourself to God.

The moment you're tempted to—

- flip through a skin magazine,
- check out online porn sites,
- fantasize about a girl at school, or
- give in to your lust in some other way

—you're faced with a choice. And the decision you make will be based on how you view yourself. If you see yourself as a slave to sin—someone who's unable to say no to your desires—you'll probably obey the commands of your lust.

If you see yourself as someone who's free from the power of sin, you'll act like a free person and walk away from the temptation. You'll demonstrate your faith with your actions. You'll trust Christ to give you the power you need to obey.

The next time lust comes calling, turn to Christ. Don't try to be an army of one and battle it alone. Don't try to ignore it and hope it will go away. Instead say a quick prayer. Thank God for giving you victory over sin. Thank him for giving you Jesus-sized power. Ask him to help you experience the victory he's given you.

If you try to fight against your lust with your own power, you don't stand a chance. It's too powerful. That's why you need to reach out to your tag-team partner. Let Christ fight the battle for you.

When I was in ninth grade, one of my classmates despised me. His name was Ron Kompton; he stood six feet, three inches tall and weighed about 230 pounds. Not the kind of enemy you want to have when you stand only five feet, nine inches tall and weigh about 130 pounds. To give you an idea of the size difference, Ron's fist was almost as large as my head.

One night at a party Ron arrived late. When he found out I was there, he hunted me down. He started calling me names and shoving me around. Like an idiot I allowed him to coax me into the front yard, where he promised to kill me.

I'd like to tell you that I reached deep within myself for

courage I didn't even know I had and scored a David-and-Goliath-like victory over my nemesis. But that's not what happened.

The truth is, I did everything but fall on my knees and cry like a baby to try and talk Ron out of beating me bloody. And I would have done that, too if I'd thought it would've save my skin.

We were standing in the yard surrounded by about 30 kids—all fight fans, eager for some violence. Suddenly a car screeched to a halt at the curb. A moment later the door slammed, and someone yelled, "Kompton!"

I recognized the voice. It was my best friend, Mike Temple. Mike was the only guy in town bigger and meaner than Ron. Mike was a two-time all-state fullback. He later played college ball for Oklahoma State. He was a tough kid who loved to fight.

Mike quickly pushed his way through the crowd. Like a classic tough guy, he walked up to Kompton and gave him a shove. "Kompton," he said, "if you're going to touch Perkins, you'll have to go through me!"

I felt a surge of courage run through me. I got into Ron's face and said, "That's right, Kompton. And don't you ever forget it."

Ron started whimpering about how he didn't know Mike and I were buddies. He promised Mike he'd never bother me again.

I like that story. Not only because I kept all my teeth that night, but also because it illustrates how Jesus fights for me. With him by my side, I don't have to worry about suffering any more humiliating defeats.

Step 4: Don't give lust a foothold.

Don't get the wrong idea. Yes, Christ gives you the power to fight the battle against lust. But having access to his power doesn't guarantee victory. You see, Christ isn't going to fight the battle for you. It's your responsibility to make sure lust doesn't get a foothold in your life.

It's easy to fall into the trap of thinking that one little sin won't hurt. That flipping through the pages of a *Playboy* is no big deal. That exchanging sexual fantasies online is harmless. However, the apostle Paul rejects that kind of thinking in Romans 6:16. Check out his warning: "Don't you know that when you offer yourselves to someone to obey him as slaves, you are slaves to the one whom you obey—whether you are slaves to sin, which leads to death, or to obedience, which leads to righteousness?"

Ultimately, by your choices you determine who will be your master. If you give your lust a small snack, it will demand more. In time it will become your master. On the other hand, if you give your life to Christ, he will be your Master.

Getting Personal

1. Have you ever been told that if you made certain changes to yourself or your lifestyle, people would like you more? If so, how do you feel about being accepted conditionally?

2. What do you remember about the transformation that occurred when you started to follow Christ?

3. What steps can you take to destroy lust's footholds in your life?

CHAPTER NINE

BREAKING THE TEMPTATION CYCLE

The Bible is, like, thousands of years old. How much help can it be for the things I'm dealing with today?
—Dewayne

Jesus said don't even think about sex when you look at a woman who's not your wife. But have you ever tried not to? There's no way.
—Bobby

There's nothing wrong with messing around. As long as you don't go too far.
—William

You're probably too young to remember the Falkland War. And unless you're a history buff, you probably know little about it. Compared to the World Wars and the Vietnam War, it was a minor skirmish. A battle for control of the Falkland Islands fought by Great Britain and Argentina back in 1982.

The British Royal Navy entered the battle with confidence. Each ship was equipped with a sophisticated defense system that identified incoming enemy missiles and shot them down before they could do any damage. In the early days of the war, the system worked flawlessly. Countless Argentine attacks were repelled without any damage to one British ship.

And then the unthinkable happened. A single missile fired from an Argentine fighter jet somehow made it past the defense system. It exploded into the hull of the *HMS Sheffield* and sank the 3,500-ton destroyer.

If that sinking came as a surprise to the British Royal Navy, the results of a later investigation into the incident must have floored them. Investigators discovered that the *Sheffield's* defense system *had* picked up the incoming missile. The ship's computer had correctly identified it as a French-made Exocet.

The problem was that the computer was programmed to ignore Exocet missiles because they were considered friendly. The computer failed to recognize that the missile had been fired from an enemy plane. So the ship was sunk by a missile it saw coming, a missile it could have destroyed.

Sometimes I feel that guys who want to be sexually pure in our hypersexual society are like giant battleships floating on the open sea. We face a constant bombardment of missiles in the form of sexual temptation, all targeted to destroy our purity.

As if that weren't bad enough, we're forced to rely on a defense system that often allows certain missiles to penetrate our minds—missiles we should see coming. Missiles we could avoid.

Let's face it. We're in hostile territory. If you're a guy living in our culture today, you can't escape the impact of being surrounded by sexual temptation. Even worse, you've got so-called experts telling you that you shouldn't *try* to escape it. They want you to believe that it's healthy to indulge your sexual appetites—no matter what those appetites include.

Wouldn't it be cool to have a foolproof defense system against sexual temptation? Maybe a force field that prevents sexual urges from reaching your brain?

Until scientists perfect an anti temptation device, the responsibility for protecting your sexual purity lies with you. You need to develop a personal defense system to help you identify and avoid the many dangerous situations our highly sexed culture throws at you.

In order to develop a system like that, though, you first have to understand what I call the temptation cycle.

The Cycle

When I was a kid, my dad once told me, "An erection has no conscience." And he was right. When a guy's lust kicks in, he loses all sense of right and wrong. He'll sacrifice anything and everything for a moment of sexual pleasure.

Your vow of commitment to God means nothing to your lust. Remember, it's a matter of who your master is. If you're controlled by your sin, you're not capable of obeying God. The apostle Paul said, "...the sinful mind is hostile to God. It does not submit to God's law, nor can it do so. Those controlled by the sinful nature cannot please God" (Romans 8:7-8).

In chapter 8, I mentioned that as long as you trust Christ to live in you, your sinful nature has no power over you. But that doesn't mean your sinful nature rolls over and dies. Oh, no. It won't go without a fight. In fact, it will never go away. It will always lurk in the shadows, looking for an opening—some kind of grip it can use to pull its way back into your life.

But there's a secret you need to know about your lust-crazed sinful nature: It's predictable. It always attacks your brain in the same way. The New Testament writer James understood that. In fact, he mapped out lust's battle plan in four stages. I call it the temptation cycle. The more you understand about those four stages, the better prepared you'll be to put up a fight.

Stage 1: Enticement

James 1:14 (NLT) says, "Temptation comes from the lure of our own evil desires." If you've ever spent any time near fresh water, you probably know that *lure* is a fishing term. James is painting a picture of a fish being drawn out of its safe area by a tempting piece of bait.

Expert fishermen know where big fish swim and how to catch them. Mark, a friend of mine, is such a fisherman. He's spent years locating the best fishing spots in the Pacific Northwest.

Early one morning my oldest son, Ryan, and I climbed into Mark's Bronco. Mark was going to show us how to catch the big ones. After driving for a few hours, we ended up by a river in the backwoods of Oregon. We hiked down a wooded trail to a rocky ledge overlooking a mountain stream.

"There are steelhead in there," Mark said, pointing to the deep, slow-moving water below us. "Bait your hooks the way I showed you and drop them in. You'll have a fish in no time."

Within a minute, Ryan's rod bent down. His reel whirred as a fish ran away with the hook. As Ryan pulled back on his rod, a three-foot steelhead arched out of the water. "Whoa, look at that!" he yelled. An hour later we'd landed four fish. Ryan's weighed almost 20 pounds.

Mark is an expert fisherman who could earn a good living as a fishing guide. He knows the right bait to drop in front of a fish to draw it out of hiding.

Unable to see the hook, a fish is captivated by the appeal of the bait. Even a granddaddy fish whose mouth is scarred from other hooks is vulnerable to the right lure.

How does a fish respond to temptation?

1. He swims around the lure.
2. He convinces himself there's no danger.
3. He persuades himself he won't get caught.
4. He tells himself he can take the bait and avoid the hook.

Sound familiar?

That's what happens to guys in the first stage of the temptation cycle. Think about it. A sexy image is dropped in front of your eyes. Maybe it's a TV commercial, bikinis on parade at the beach, or a poster on your friend's bedroom wall.

Whatever the image is, it's a lure—something to make your lustful nature sit up and say, "Wow, that looks good. Wouldn't you like some of that? Go for it. After all, that's what guys do."

The goal, of course, is to lure you out of your safety area. To get you to fall for the lies of your lust. To make you convince yourself that you can play with the bait and not get hooked.

This is the stage where you need to wage your most intense battle. You need to catch yourself daydreaming about porn. Or fantasizing about a girl in your neighborhood. Or anything else that stirs up your lust. You need to learn to switch mental gears in a heartbeat.

If you're looking for an example of the perfect way to handle the first stage of the temptation cycle, head on over to Matthew 4 in your Bible. That's where you'll find the story of Satan tempting Jesus in the wilderness.

Obviously Satan is a pro's pro when it comes to temptation. He knew exactly where to attack Jesus. Jesus hadn't eaten for 40 days. So Satan tempted him to turn stones into bread. He tried to take advantage of Jesus' intense need for food.

No one would've blamed Jesus for at least considering Satan's idea. Imagine how hungry he must've been. But Jesus didn't give the temptation time to settle in his brain. If you read the story, you'll notice there's no gap between Satan's temptation and the Lord's reply. Jesus immediately quoted Scripture to slam the door on Satan's attack.

That's the kind of mental alertness you need to defend yourself against sexual temptation. "Therefore, prepare your minds for action; be self-controlled; set your hope fully on the grace to be given you when Jesus Christ is revealed." Those are the apostle Peter's words of advice in 1 Peter 1:13.

If you want to cut off temptation at the enticement stage— and believe me, you do—you need to be prepared. You need to be self-controlled. And you need to be focused on Christ.

There's no better way to equip yourself for battle than by memorizing Scripture. The Bible was Jesus' weapon of choice against Satan's temptations. And if it's good enough for him, it's certainly good enough for us.

I've found that memorizing large sections of the Bible gives me a safe thing to focus on when I'm tempted. By the time I recite a few verses to myself, my spirit is strengthened and my mind is cleared.

God uses the Bible to expose the danger of the bait. To a fish, a lure looks like real food. It gives the illusion of being something it's not. In a similar way, the object of our lust gives the illusion of intimacy. Not only does it give us pleasure, but it also promises to fill the emptiness inside us. Memorizing the truth of Scripture helps us to see the illusion for what it really is.

An added benefit of memorizing Scripture is the fact that you can only concentrate on one thing at a time. As long as you're mentally reviewing Bible verses, your mind doesn't have time for sexual joyrides.

Stage 2: Conception

James 1:15 tells us that "...after desire has conceived, it gives birth to sin." Notice that James changes his imagery from fishing to maternity. The idea here is that our lustful thoughts are given life. The seeds that were planted by temptation start to take root and grow.

The bad news is that once your lust reaches this stage, it usually can't be stopped. This is where the rituals start. Remember the rituals we talked about earlier in the book? They're the things you do before you actually carry out a sexual sin.

In the Lord's Prayer, Jesus teaches us to ask God to deny us the opportunity to sin when we have the desire. You see, when the opportunity to sin and the desire to sin come together, we're in trouble.

You may not always be able to control your desires, but you can control the opportunities you face. You do that by getting rid of your rituals. It's crucial during times of strength and sanity that you protect yourself from times when you're weak.

Depending on which way your lust carries you, your rituals may include things like—

- surfing the Internet,
- browsing in a video store,
- calling a girl you know you can score with,
- channel surfing late at night, or
- checking out commercials for "intimate" 1-900 numbers.

Each of us has unique rituals. And if you're serious about breaking free from your sexual lust, you need to identify your rituals. Make a list of the things you do to build the anticipation and to increase the pleasure of your sexual compulsions. Be honest and thorough in creating your list. Don't leave anything out.

Once your list is complete, you need to brainstorm ways to remove those rituals from your life. This is where you need to be ruthless. Do whatever you have to do to keep yourself away from your rituals. Holding on to even one ritual will keep your lust alive and ready to attack.

If you have a TV in your bedroom, take it out. Refuse to watch TV after 10 p.m. unless your parents are in the room.

Keep your bedroom door open at all times. Stay away from the magazine rack when you go to the store. Uncover (for your parents to see) your hiding places for porn. Go to www.millionmightymen.com and click on the "Covenant Eyes" tab. Covenant Eyes offers software that keeps a non-erasable record of every site your computer visits. It then e-mails that record to two accountability partners (perhaps your youth leader and a trusted Christian friend). Knowing that someone else is seeing the sites you visit is a great deterrent to surfing for porn.

If those ideas seem a little extreme—or unnecessary—to you, you may be underestimating the power of rituals. And if you do that, you're headed straight for Stage 3.

Stage 3: Birth

You know about the birds and the bees. So you know that birth naturally follows conception. As far as your lust is concerned, if you dream about something long enough—if you make plans for it—you will carry it out eventually. You'll make a grab for the bait.

Stage 4: Death

James 1:15 explains how the cycle is completed: "Then, after desire has conceived, it gives birth to sin; and sin, when it is full-grown, gives birth to death." That's not what your lust tells you now, of course. Your lust promises life, joy, pleasure, and intimacy. But that's never how things work out.

Instead of life, lust brings death. Instead of joy, lust brings shame. Instead of pleasure, lust brings pain. Instead of intimacy, lust brings the illusion of intimacy.

Sinful sexual behavior always ends badly. Ask King David.

After his affair with Bathsheba, he murdered her husband. Later the child that was born from the affair died.

Ask Samson. After his affair with Delilah, he lost his sight and sacrificed his position as a leader of Israel.

Ask the men whose names appear in the newspaper as targets of a prostitution sting. They sacrificed their families and reputations because they didn't say no to their lust.

Nobody escapes the consequences of sexual compulsion. Nobody! There's a high price to be paid for disobeying God with your body. Unfortunately, most guys don't discover that until it's too late.

Don't be a casualty. A victim of your uncontrollable lust. Use what you know about the temptation cycle to break lust's power over you. Stay away from the lure, no matter how tempting it looks. Save yourself the pain of the hook.

Getting Personal

1. When was the last time your lust made you forget about your commitment to God? How did you feel about your commitment afterward?

2. How many Bible verses do you know by heart? Name three verses you think might be helpful in your battle against sexual temptation.

3. What ritual will be the most difficult for you to eliminate from your life? What will you have to do in order to finally get rid of it?

CHAPTER TEN

NEGOTIATING TIGHT CORNERS

I was so good for, like, a month. And then one day I got bored and—well, you know. I'll never have a streak like that again.
—Mark

I know God's forgiven me for the stuff I've done, but I still feel like scum when I think about it.
—Chris

It's impossible not to think about sex all the time.
—Omar

My neighbor Ernie is a tool freak. His garage is a handyman's paradise. Tools galore. Every size, make, and model. If it can be used for construction or repair, chances are Ernie owns it.

Several years ago I discovered just how useful Ernie's tool collection was. My plan was to take out our old kitchen faucet and replace it with a new one. As I confidently snapped a fitting onto the end of a socket wrench, I told myself the job would take 30 minutes, tops. After all, it was a simple procedure. What could possibly slow me down?

Turns out that the tiny space between the back of the sink and the wall did just that. I tried every possible angle, but I couldn't get the end of the wrench over the head of the nut that was holding the fixture in place.

As you might imagine, it wasn't one of the most spiritual experiences of my life. (If you've ever had to deal with a frustrating situation like that, you know what I'm talking about.) Just as I was about to give up and do the unthinkable—call a plumber—I remembered Ernie and his tool emporium across the street.

Ernie smiled when I explained my problem to him. "I have a set of plumber's tools made exactly for that job," he said. He pulled an unopened box from the top of a shelf in his garage and handed it to me. "It's a set of wrench extensions," he explained. "You'll be the first to use them. I knew they'd come in handy one day!"

Three minutes later I had the first nut off. Suddenly a job that had seemed impossible became a breeze. The right tool solved the problem created by a tight corner.

Your Tool Chest

You're not naive. You know that if you commit yourself to being sexually pure, you're going to face some tough times. Occasionally you're going to find yourself in a tight corner, and no matter how hard you try, you won't be able to work your way out of it.

Temptation, disappointment, doubt, and setbacks may start you worrying that you're not going to succeed in your quest to be pure. If things get really bad, you might even be tempted to throw in the towel and say, "Forget it."

That's when this chapter will come in handy. Think of the last few pages of this book as a toolbox. It's filled with tools designed to help you work your way out of tight corners. As you read these pages, mark the tools you think will be useful for you. You'll want to be able to find them quickly when you need them later.

Tools

A Calendar

One day at a time. That's how you have to approach your commitment to being sexually pure. You can't think about quitting your sexual sins for a year. Or a month. Or even a week. You have to start each new day with a fresh commitment. You have to tell yourself that you will not feed your lust for the next 24 hours. And when that time period's up, you have to do the same thing again.

While you're doing that, you can monitor your progress with a calendar. If you successfully complete a day without giving in to your lust, mark it on your calendar. If you stumble or relapse, indicate that on your calendar, too. And try to be as specific as possible about the circumstances that triggered your fall.

Over time you may begin to see a pattern of temptation that occurs at specific times of the week, month, or year. You may also start to notice particular situations that entice you more than others.

Once you see the patterns of your life recorded on your calendar, you'll be able to anticipate times when you're most vulnerable. And if you can anticipate heavy temptation, you can prepare yourself for it and figure out ways to cope with it more effectively.

Safeguards Against Rituals

Remember the lists you made in chapter 9? The ones where you identified the rituals that lead to your sexual sin and then brainstormed ways to avoid them? You need to keep those lists handy.

If you're serious about overcoming your compulsive sexual behavior, you need safeguards in place. You have to be able to recognize the circumstances, conversations, and relationships that trigger your lust. And for every trigger you identify, you need a safeguard: a way of defusing it: a plan for removing it from your life.

Healthy Self-Talk

The worse you feel about yourself, the better chance lust has of running free in your life. So you can bet your sinful nature is going to try to fill your mind with shame and self-hatred. Don't let it.

Combat your negative thoughts with healthy, Bible-based

self-talk. If you're not sure how to do that, start by repeating this phrase out loud throughout the day: "God unconditionally loves me, and I receive his love and accept myself."

The more you say it, the sooner you'll believe it. The sooner you believe it, the sooner you'll act like it's true.

A Support Person

There's an old saying: *No man is an island.* God doesn't intend for us to live in isolation. He made us social creatures. Whether we admit it or not, we need other people's input in our lives. On top of that, those of us who struggle with sexual compulsions have a responsibility to care for and support each other.

You need a friend who will love and accept you. A friend who will pray for you. A friend who will speak the truth to you. You need a friend you can share your darkest secrets with. A friend you can trust not to reveal those secrets. You need a friend who won't walk away in disgust when he hears what you've done. But you also need a friend who won't let you off too easy when it comes to taking responsibility for your actions. You need a friend who's a mature believer in Christ. A friend who knows the Bible. A friend who knows what it means to struggle with lust—and win.

If you have no one in your life who can fill that role for you, talk to a male church leader. He may be able to hook you up with someone who can help you. Or he may volunteer to fill that role himself.

Once you have your support person in place, talk to him. Speak openly about your struggles and failures. Help him understand your rituals. Give him the information he needs to help you avoid them. Remember, the more open and honest you are, the more your support person can help you.

Patient Hope

Don't forget that you've signed up for a marathon, not a sprint. After a few days or weeks of staying pure, you can expect your lust to come roaring back with a vengeance. Sexual compulsion is a problem that takes a long time—sometimes even a lifetime—to overcome.

If you know that ahead of time, you can avoid the discouragement and depression that often come when you have a setback. If you really want to do yourself a favor, memorize Isaiah's words of encouragement in Isaiah 40:31: "...those who hope in the Lord will renew their strength. They will soar on wings like eagles; they will run and not grow weary, they will walk and not be faint."

Pain

Pain isn't your enemy. Not when you're trying to break free from your sexual lust. In fact, pain is a tool that can make you stronger. Remember—running from pain (of some kind or another) is probably what left you vulnerable to your compulsion in the first place. The more you tried to bury your pain, the deeper you sank into lust.

Instead of running from your pain, ride it out like you would a rising tide. Eventually your craving to bury your pain with sex will recede. And you'll be a little stronger the next time the tide comes in.

If it's any consolation, you can remind yourself that no one makes it through this life without his share of pain. Look at Paul's description of his intense pain (or, as he called it, "a thorn in my flesh") in 2 Corinthians 12:7-9. We don't know for sure what caused Paul's pain, but we know he suffered tremendously. Three times he begged God to take his pain away. And three times God refused—because he had a better plan. Instead of removing the cause of Paul's pain, God gave him extra grace to endure it.

And how did Paul respond to God's plan? See for yourself in 2 Corinthians 12:9-10: "...I will boast all the more gladly about my weaknesses, so that Christ's power may rest on me. That is why, for Christ's sake, I delight in weaknesses, in insults, in hardships, in persecutions, in difficulties. For when I am weak, then I am strong."

Paul learned how to rely on God's grace when he was suffering. His pain didn't go away—but his strength and endurance increased. And that was more than enough help for him.

That same grace is available to you. When you're hurting, ask God to give you the grace you need to endure. Ask him to show you his strength in your weakness.

A Consequences and Benefits List

Remember the lists you made in chapter 7? The ones where you spelled out the consequences of giving in to your lust and the benefits of being sexually pure? You need to keep those lists handy. You need to be able to refer to them when you feel yourself starting to slip. You need to be able to see for yourself that the pleasure of giving in to your lust lasts only for a few minutes, but the consequences may last a lifetime.

Tears

Crying isn't something most guys do in public (except maybe professional athletes who are announcing their retirement).

Some guys don't even cry in private. They view tears as a sign of weakness. They consider crying to be a feminine thing to do.

That's a shame. Tears clean the body and soul. If you hold them back, you create a dam in your emotional stream. And that stream needs to flow freely to keep your heart pure.

Jesus wasn't too hard-core to cry. When he saw his friends Mary and Martha weeping after the death of their brother Lazarus, he cried, too.

As you think about the hurt you've suffered in your life, you may need to cry. Disappointment can take a heavy toll. So let your emotions flow. God understands. As you cry, imagine Jesus wrapping his arms around you.

Forgiveness

Forgiveness is like the Phillips screwdriver of this toolbox. You're going to need it often. There are three dimensions of forgiveness you're going to need to use.

1. Finding forgiveness

No matter what you've done or how many times you've done it, God offers you forgiveness. No sin is too perverted or too offensive to disqualify you from his forgiveness.

If God has forgiven you, you need to forgive yourself. Don't keep beating yourself up over past sins. Remember: Jesus paid for your sins with his life. He took the punishment you deserve. Three days later he rose from the dead, leaving your guilt and shame buried forever. Why would you want to dig it up again?

2. Offering forgiveness

Once you've received God's forgiveness, you have a responsibility to forgive the people who've hurt you. Otherwise it's like saying your standards are higher than God's. And that's never a good idea.

Forgiving the people who've caused your pain is a tough thing to do, especially if your wounds are deep and open. But those wounds will never heal until you clean them out by forgiving the people who caused them.

"Some things can't be forgiven," you might say. "You don't understand what they've done to me."

You're right. I don't understand. I'm sorry you've been hurt. But if you've read about the last few days of Jesus' life in Scripture—or seen *The Passion of the Christ*—you know you haven't been brutalized more than Jesus was on the day of his crucifixion. Yet in Luke 23:34 he offered forgiveness to those who killed him.

There's a difference between forgiveness and reconciliation. Reconciliation can only occur when the person who's caused the pain realizes exactly what he's done and seeks forgiveness. Even if reconciliation doesn't occur, you still need to forgive. You may forgive someone and never be reconciled with him.

Once you've asked God to forgive the people who've hurt you, each time you remember the hurt, pray for those people. There's no better way than prayer to get rid of bitterness and grudges.

3. Seeking forgiveness

If you've hurt others while satisfying your lust, you need to ask forgiveness from them. Before you do that, though, you need to think through what you'll say. Don't just toss off a quick "My bad" and let it go at that. Be honest and get straight to the point. Say something like, "I see that I've hurt you by _____. I'm very sorry. Will you forgive me?"

I can't guarantee that you'll receive forgiveness. People who've been hurt are often suspicious of apologies and attempts to reconcile. Some people may tell you flat out that they won't forgive you. If that happens, don't try to argue or persuade them. Just tell them you understand and ask them to pray for you.

Bible Meditations

This is a personal favorite of mine. Nothing helps me stay sexually pure like memorizing and meditating on Bible verses that deal with my feelings and struggles. Try it yourself. If you're not sure where to start, here's a top 10 list of possibilities.

Temptation

"No temptation has seized you except what is common to man. And God is faithful; he will not let you be tempted beyond what you can bear. But when you are tempted, he will also provide a way out so that you can stand up under it" (1 Corinthians 10:13).

"Blessed is the man who perseveres under trial, because when he has stood the test, he will receive the crown of life that God has promised to those who love him. When tempted, no one should say, 'God is tempting me.' For God cannot be tempted by evil, nor does he tempt anyone; but each one is tempted when, by his own evil desire, he is dragged away and enticed. Then, after desire has conceived, it gives birth to sin; and sin, when it is full-grown, gives birth to death" (James 1:12-15).

Anxiety

"Do not be anxious about anything, but in everything, by prayer and petition, with thanksgiving, present your requests to God. And the peace of God, which transcends all understanding, will guard your hearts and your minds in Christ Jesus" (Philippians 4:6-7).

Nasty thoughts

"Finally, brothers, whatever is true, whatever is noble, whatever is right, whatever is pure, whatever is lovely, whatever is admirable—if anything is excellent or praiseworthy—think about such things" (Philippians 4:8).

Lust

"Flee from sexual immorality. All other sins a man commits are outside his body, but he who sins sexually sins against his own body" (1 Corinthians 6:18).

Forgiveness

"If we confess our sins, he is faithful and just and will forgive us our sins and purify us from all unrighteousness" (1 John 1:9).

Prayer

"The Lord is near to all who call on him, to all who call on him in truth" (Psalm 145:18).

"Ask and it will be given to you; seek and you will find; knock and the door will be opened to you. For everyone who asks receives; he who seeks finds; and to him who knocks, the door will be opened" (Matthew 7:7-8).

Self-image

"Therefore, if anyone is in Christ, he is a new creation; the old has gone, the new has come!" (2 Corinthians 5:17)

"I have been crucified with Christ and I no longer live, but Christ lives in me. The life I live in the body, I live by faith in the Son of God, who loved me and gave himself for me" (Galatians 2:20).

Prayer

Prayer is simply talking with God. It's the way you stay connected to the One who gives you his love and forgiveness. The One who gives you the power you need to control your lust.

You can do yourself an enormous favor by carving out a chunk of time every day to spend in one-on-one dialogue with God. Earlier in the book we saw that lust offers the illusion of intimacy. And guys who are looking for intimacy try to find it in empty sexual experiences.

Prayer time with God offers a chance for *real* intimacy. Every time you pray, he gives you an opportunity to draw close to him. And the more you experience real intimacy, the less likely you are to go chasing after the false kind.

Journaling

Keeping a journal is a tangible way to measure your progress (and your setbacks) in your battle against lust. Set aside a few minutes every day to write down some of the key events of the day. Be sure to make a note of your successes and failures in keeping your lust in check. You might also consider including a prayer in each day's entry. That way you'll have something to look back on when your prayers are answered.

A Final Warning

I wish I could offer you a guarantee that if you take the tips and suggestions in this book to heart, you'll never stumble in your quest to be sexually pure. But I can't.

I can tell you that you must never let a stumble become the final chapter of your story. Resist the urge to say, "Now that I've blown it, I might as well quit trying." Learn from your mistake. Then start your comeback.

You can do it. You can live a sexually pure life. You can overcome sexual temptations. You can defeat your lust. Because God is on your side.

Getting Personal

1. Which tools do you think will be most useful to you? Why?

2. Who are the leading candidates to serve as your support person? What qualifies each one to be a potential support person for you?

3. After reading this book, what are your thoughts about living a sexually pure life?